SNARE DRUM
BY BEN HANS

MW00934893

ISBN: 9798883345110
COPYRIGHT © 2024 BEN HANS & TROY NELSON MUSIC LLC
International Copyright Secured. All Rights Reserved.

HOW TO GET THE AUDIO

The audio files for this book are available to download or stream for free on *troynelsonmusic.com*.

We are available to help you with your audio downloads and any other questions you may have. Simply email *help@troynelsonmusic.com*.

See below for the recommended ways to listen to the audio:

Download Audio Files

- Download Audio Files (Zipped)

- Recommended for COMPUTERS on WiFi

- A ZIP file will automatically download to the default "downloads" folder on your computer

- Recommended: download to a desktop/laptop computer *first*, then transfer to a tablet or cell phone

- Phones & tablets may need an "unzipping" app such as iZip, Unrar, or Winzip

- Download on WiFi for faster download speeds

Stream Audio Files

- Recommended for CELL PHONES & TABLETS

- Bookmark this page

- Simply tap the PLAY button on the track you want to listen to

- Files also available for streaming or download at: *soundcloud.com/troynelsonbooks*

To download the companion audio files for this book, visit: troynelsonmusic.com/audio-downloads/

INTRODUCTION

Welcome to *Snare Drum 365*! Come join me and drum! As the title implies, I want you to play every day! Inside this book are 365 snare drum drills, one for each day of an entire year. Concepts such as *rhythm*, *rudiments*, *time signatures*, *dynamics*, and *drum-tone variations* are covered throughout the book to help you develop musicianship and musicality. All of this culminates in a drum solo on Day 365!

To become a better player, you must dedicate time each day to growth on your instrument. Granted, as you get deeper into the book, some figures and patterns may take longer than one practice session to complete. That's OK! The real challenge is to play every day, not to prefect the material in one session. And by purchasing this book, you've accepted that challenge!

My hope is that this book will be of great help to you as a drum student, no matter your skill level, and it will provide fun, interesting, and effective material for your individual sessions or sessions with a drum instructor. In fact, if you have difficulty with the material in this book, I recommend that you seek out a professional drum instructor in your area for some mentoring.

If you have any questions about the material in this book, please reach out to me via my website, *benhans.com*.

Happy Drumming!

Ben

Dedication and Credits

This book is dedicated to my late friend, mentor, teacher, inspiration, and "Drum Dad," John S. "Jack" Pratt.

All audio tracks performed by the author on a Yamaha Oak Custom 14" x 5.5" Snare Drum and a Yamaha SFZ Marching Snare Drum, both equipped with Aquarian Reflector Series batter heads, with Vic Firth SD1 Generals and Vic Firth MS2 Marching Snare sticks.

All audio tracks recorded by Kevin White at SAE Institute Nashville (Studio A), on September 24th and October 9th, 2023.

NOTATION LEGEND

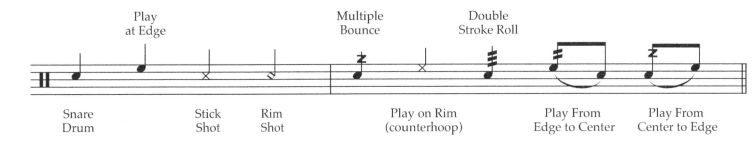

WEEK 1: QUARTER NOTES

MONDAY   1

This exercise features eight strokes per hand, as well as alternate sticking in the third and fourth examples. Alternating hands at a very fast rate of speed will give you the sound of the Single Stroke Roll rudiment.

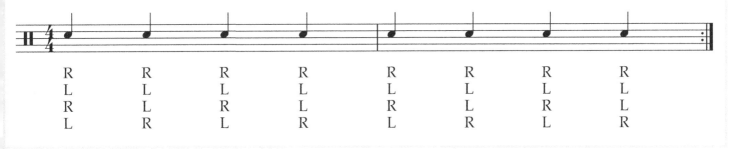

TUESDAY   2

Here, we have two strokes in each hand. When your technique improves, you'll discover that this sticking becomes the Double Stroke Roll. Start with the right-hand lead, then try the left-hand lead.

WEDNESDAY   3

This sticking pattern is the Single Paradiddle.

THURSDAY

Here, we have the Double Paradiddle rudiment over three bars, with a Single Paradiddle on the turnaround.

FRIDAY

This sticking pattern is the Triple Paradiddle.

SATURDAY

Here, we have the Paradiddle-Diddle. Practice the repeats with the right-hand lead. When comfortable, try the left-hand lead.

SUNDAY

This sticking pattern is the Triple Stroke Roll rudiment in fundamental quarter notes. When your technique improves, this pattern will become a roll.

WEEK 1 SUMMARY EXERCISE

In this summary exercise, the Single Paradiddle is followed by the Double Paradiddle and, finally, the Paradiddle-Diddle. Use a right-hand lead. When comfortable, flip the sticking to a left-hand lead.

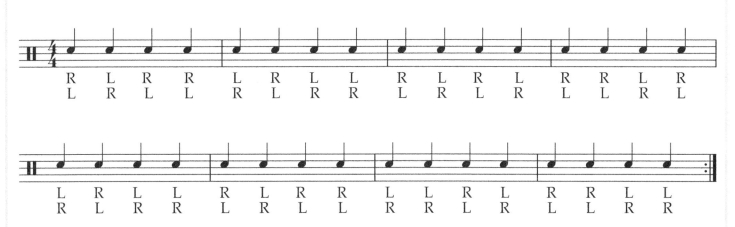

WEEK 2: EIGHTH NOTES

MONDAY 8

Here's an eighth-note reading exercises phrased in a two-bar pattern. Make sure to count aloud: "1-and, 2-and, 3-and, 4-and," etc.

TUESDAY 9

Alternate stick the exercises with a right-hand lead, then practice the left-hand lead.

WEDNESDAY 10

Make sure to keep counting aloud while practicing.

THURSDAY 11

If you alternate stick this exercise, it will naturally move to the left-hand lead on the repeat.

FRIDAY 12

Here's another exercise that will move to the left hand on the repeat.

SATURDAY 13

I'm counting on you to count. Are you?

SUNDAY 14

Make sure to alternate the sticking and practice with a metronome.

WEEK 2 SUMMARY EXERCISE

This eight-bar exercise contains variations from this week's exercises, as well as a few new variations. Make sure to count while playing!

WEEK 3: EIGHTH NOTES & RESTS

MONDAY 15

This exercise is an introduction to the eighth-note rest. Make sure to count and practice with a metronome.

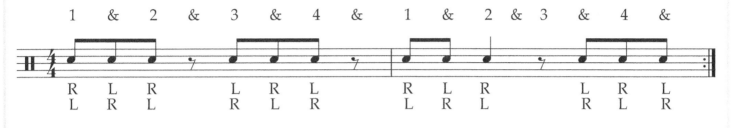

TUESDAY 16

Count out loud while practicing.

WEDNESDAY 17

Continue to count and alternate-stick.

THURSDAY

How's your technique as you're playing? Continue to work on it as you practice. Performing in front of a mirror will help.

FRIDAY

Be cautious with the downbeat eighth-note rest.

SATURDAY

Having trouble here? Get out that metronome!

SUNDAY

Still counting? Aloud?

WEEK 3 SUMMARY EXERCISE

This 16-bar exercise contains variations from this week's exercises, as well as new variations. Make sure to count while playing! Try playing at 60 beats per minute (BPM) and then increase by 8–10 BPM as you get more comfortable with the patterns.

WEEK 4: 16TH NOTES

MONDAY 22

This exercise introduces the 16th note. Count 16th notes like this: "1-e-&-ah, 2-e-&-ah," etc.

TUESDAY 23

This exercise is a mix of quarter-note and 16th-note groupings.

WEDNESDAY 24

Similar to yesterday's exercise, this pattern features eighth notes on beats 1 and 3.

THURSDAY

Don't forget to work on your timing with a metronome.

FRIDAY

Play very slowly at first. As you feel more comfortable with the pattern, increase your speed.

SATURDAY

Notice the space between the quarter notes versus the eighth notes in previous exercises.

SUNDAY

Lots of 16th notes in this one. Make sure you're playing everything in time.

WEEK 4 SUMMARY EXERCISE

This eight-bar exercise contains variations from this week's exercises, as well as some new variations. Remember to count while playing these exercises. Have fun!

WEEK 5: 16TH-NOTE VARIATIONS

MONDAY 29

Here's an introduction to eighth- and 16th-note patterns.

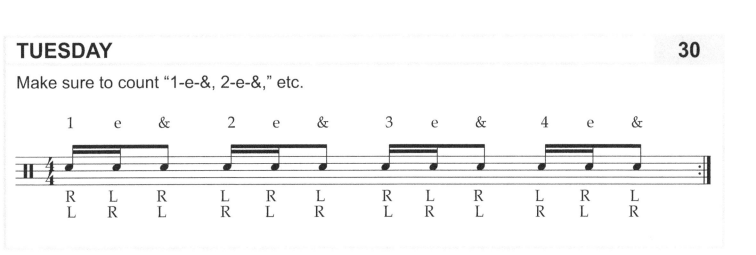

TUESDAY 30

Make sure to count "1-e-&, 2-e-&," etc.

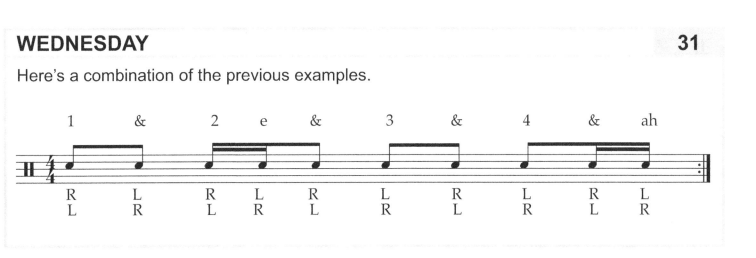

WEDNESDAY 31

Here's a combination of the previous examples.

THURSDAY

32

A metronome will help you here!

FRIDAY

33

Don't let the shapes of the rhythms fool you! Say it and you can play it!

SATURDAY

34

Watch out for these combinations—they can be tricky at first.

SUNDAY

35

Counting aloud is key. Don't forget or get lazy.

WEEK 5 SUMMARY EXERCISE

This 16-bar exercise contains variations from this week's exercises, as well as new variations. You absolutely need to count while playing these exercises! Watch out for the eighth-note rests in bars 11 and 13!

MONDAY 36

Today, we're going to try some exercises in 2/4 time. In other words, just two quarter-note beats per measure.

TUESDAY 37

Again, just counting to 2 here. The rhythms should be familiar by now.

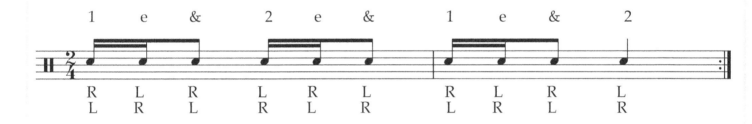

WEDNESDAY 38

Here's another exercise in 2/4 time.

Now, we're switching to 3/4 time, with a three-quarter-note beat pulse.

Simply count in 3, and you'll have this one in no time.

Count in 3!

Here's a good combination of 16th-note patterns. It's good practice to work on both your right-hand lead and your left-hand lead. Make sure to play even strokes with both hands.

WEEK 6 SUMMARY EXERCISE

Here are three eight-bar examples in 2/4 and 3/4 time. The metronome will be a great ally here!

EX. 1   1   2 e & ah   1   &   2   & ah   1   &   2 e & ah   *simile*

EX. 2   1   & ah 2 & 3   *simile*

EX. 3

WEEK 7: MULTIPLE STROKE ROLL

MONDAY

What we want to produce here is a Multiple Bounce on the quarter-note pulse. Notice the "Z" on the stem, which is used to notate the Multiple Bounce.

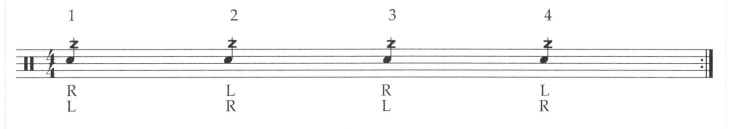

TUESDAY

Today, we want to expand on the Multiple Bounce technique and run it together in an eighth-note pulse. Don't let any space occur between your alternate stokes; instead, strive for a consistent pulse and constant sound.

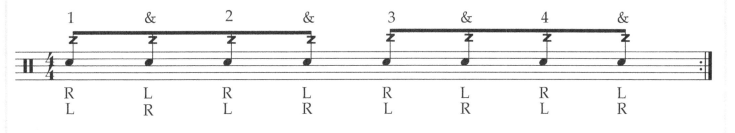

WEDNESDAY

Here is the primer for a Five Stroke Roll. We'll first work on it with the Multiple Bounce technique. You'll want to perfect the sound of this for nice, concert-style snare rolls.

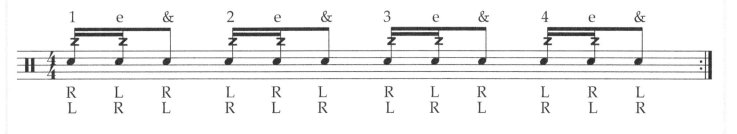

THURSDAY

46

Same approach as yesterday but we're starting the Multiple Bounce on the "and" of each beat.

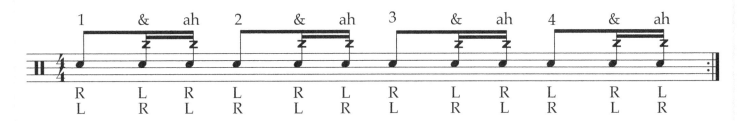

FRIDAY

47

Here is the transition to the notation for a concert-style Multiple Bounce Roll. For now, we'll use the 16th-note pulse.

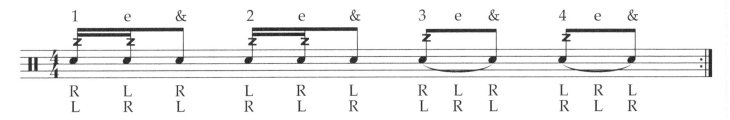

SATURDAY

48

Here's another illustration moving toward concert-style roll notation.

Now, we'll add the accent. An accent note is played louder than the others. Perform the accent with a firmer downstroke. An accent is illustrated by the "greater than" sign (>), which is placed above the note.

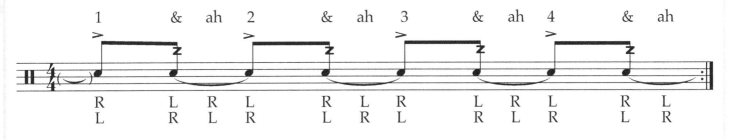

WEEK 7 SUMMARY EXERCISE

This eight-bar exercise contains rolls from this week's exercises. Make sure to play an even-handed roll throughout this exercise.

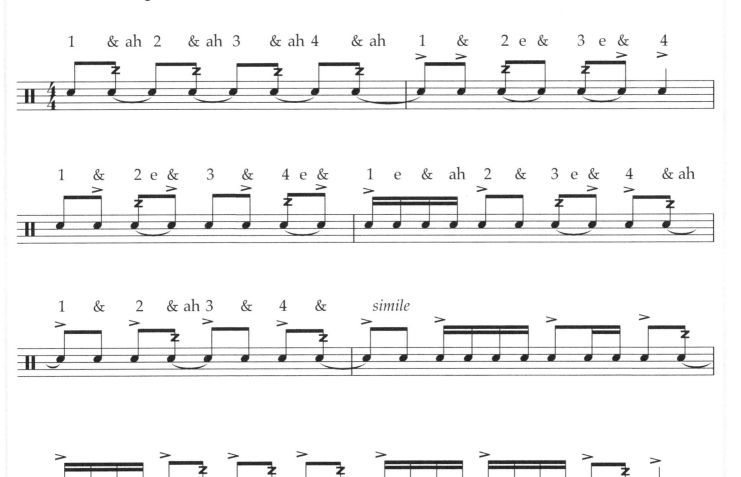

MONDAY   50

Today, we introduce the 16th-note rest. If you count all your 16th notes, you can't go wrong! Just be silent on the rests.

TUESDAY   51

The rhythms in the next two examples are notated two different ways but are performed exactly the same on the drum. On other instruments, musicians can acknowledge the 16th-note rest, but since the snare drum has such a staccato sound (i.e., very little sustain), there's no tangible difference between the two notated rhythms.

WEDNESDAY   52

Make sure to count these examples: "1-e-ah, 2-e-ah," etc.

Again, no discernable difference on the snare drum between the two notated rhythms. If you were to sing the note values, however, you'd notice the difference. Try it! Hold out the eighth note, then cut the note short to acknowledge the 16th-note rest.

Whoa, whoa, whoa! Sixteenth-note rests on the downbeats?! Be careful! Count it, and you'll get it!

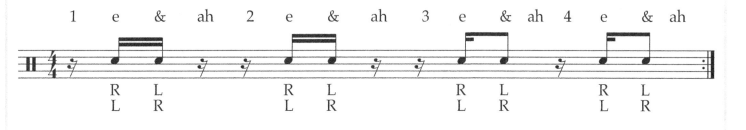

Count all the 16th notes in this exercise and play the figure precisely.

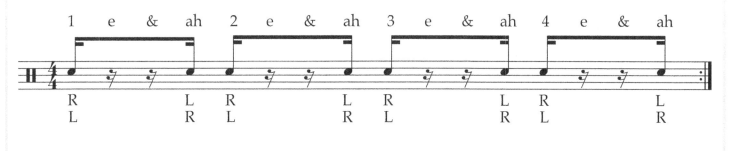

There are lots of syncopated, offbeat pulses here. Try this one with your metronome!

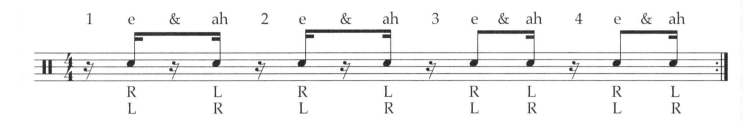

WEEK 8 SUMMARY EXERCISE

This eight-bar exercise contains variations from this week's exercises. In other words, business as usual. Count and play with the metronome.

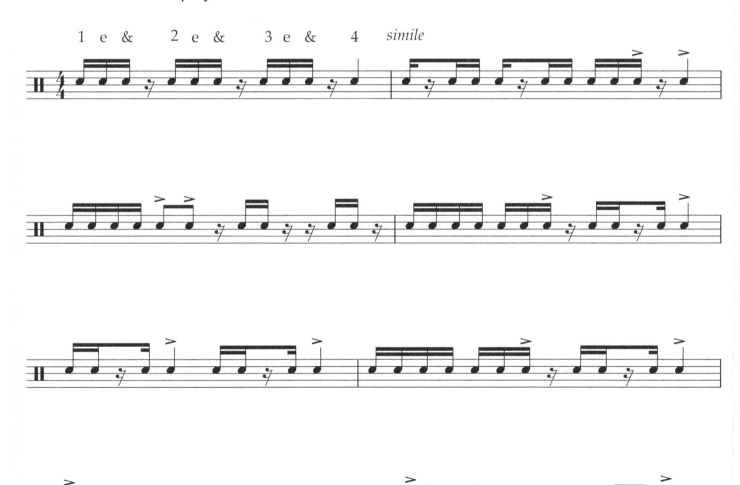

WEEK 9: DOTTED RHYTHMS

MONDAY 57

This week, we'll look at half notes and dotted notes. Half notes receive two quarter-note beat pulses. A dot increases the note value by one half, so the dotted half note receives three quarter-note beats.

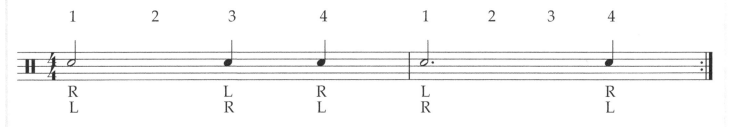

TUESDAY 58

In bar 2, we have a dotted quarter note. The dot increases the note by one half, so the dotted quarter note receives three eighth-note beats. On the snare drum, the dot has the same feel as an eighth-note rest, as in the first measure. Winds, strings, and vocals, however, will sustain the dotted note.

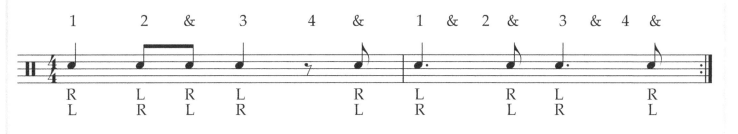

WEDNESDAY 59

Count all these rhythms!

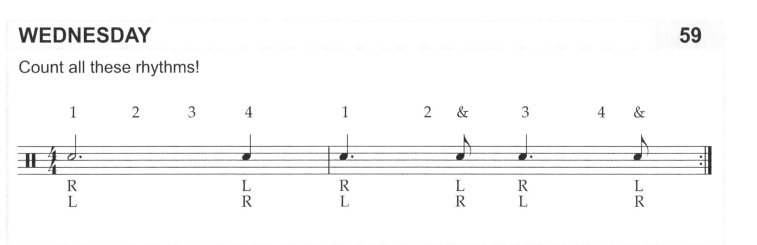

THURSDAY

Today, we encounter the dotted eighth note. Dotted eighth notes receive three 16th-note beat pulses. Use the metronome and set it to an eighth-note pulse—or even a 16th-note pulse if you have trouble feeling these rhythms.

FRIDAY

There are dotted 16th notes galore in this exercise. Make sure to play accurate subdivisions.

SATURDAY

Count, count, count!

Notice the different feel of the dotted 16ths and dotted quarters in this exericse.

WEEK 9 SUMMARY EXERCISE

Here is a 12-bar exercise. Practice with a metronome to make sure your phrasing is correct. Have fun!

WEEK 10: THE FLAM & THE DRAG

MONDAY

The Flam is a drum rudiment whose main note is preceded by a grace note. The Flam is often hard for a beginner to execute correctly. Here's a tip: "Flam" is an onomatopoeia, so say it aloud to get the right feel: "Flaaa - mmm." In today's example, the left-hand grace note is a tap stroke, and the right hand is a full stroke. Vice versa on the left-hand lead.

TUESDAY

Today, we'll alternate the Flam: left-hand tap and right-hand downstroke, followed by the right-hand tap and left-hand downstroke. Eventually, the tap will evolve into an upstroke. This will make the flam very simple for you to play and it will sound great every time.

WEDNESDAY

Here are some Flams in 3/4 time.

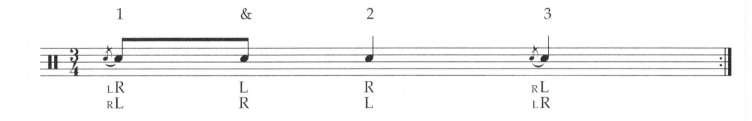

THURSDAY

Today, we're going to try the Single Drag. Play two grace notes before the main note.

FRIDAY

This exercise features the Single Drag and Flam together! Notice the different feel of the figures.

SATURDAY

Some more 3/4 phrasing today.

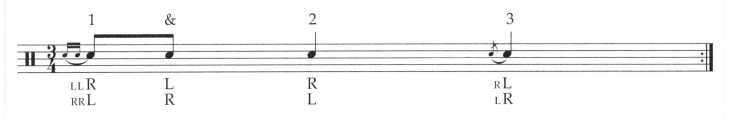

SUNDAY

Today, we'll learn the alternating Three Stroke Ruff. To perform this rudiment, alternate two taps before the main note. This is a great figure to master and a great sticking pattern to use on the drum set!

WEEK 10 SUMMARY EXERCISE

Make sure to execute clean grace notes in this eight-bar exercise.

MONDAY 71

As always, remember to count aloud and practice with your metronome!

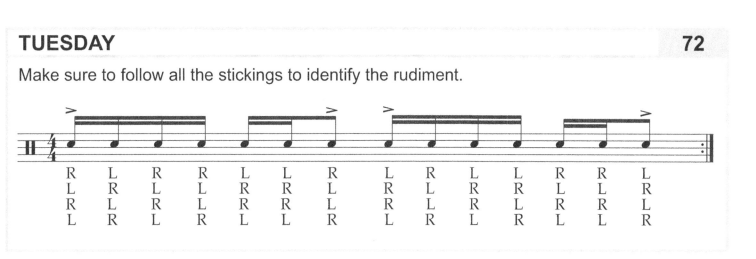

TUESDAY 72

Make sure to follow all the stickings to identify the rudiment.

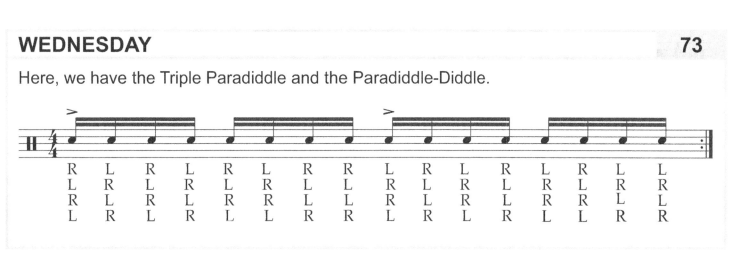

WEDNESDAY 73

Here, we have the Triple Paradiddle and the Paradiddle-Diddle.

THURSDAY

Be sure to follow the stickings in this exercise.

FRIDAY

Lots of syncopated rhythms here. Counting is a must.

SATURDAY

Even more syncopations for you here. Watch out!

SUNDAY

How 'bout a little Five Stroke Roll review?

WEEK 11 SUMMARY EXERCISE

This 16-bar exercise contains a mixture of examples from the previous weeks' exercises.

WEEK 12: THE FIVE STROKE ROLL

MONDAY 78

Here is a primer for Open Rolls.

TUESDAY 79

Today's example is a preparatory exercise for the Five Stroke Roll.

WEDNESDAY 80

Using the previous examples, phrase the open Five Stroke Roll between two eighth-note beat pulses.

THURSDAY

Today, you'll be phrasing the Five Stroke Roll on the "and" of beats 3 and 4.

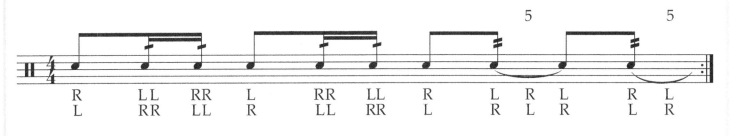

FRIDAY

Make sure to alternate your sticking here to work on your left-handed Five Stroke Rolls.

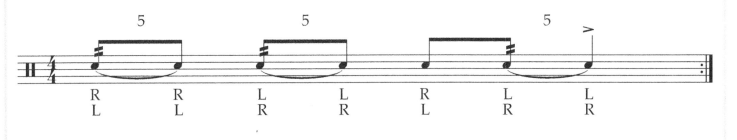

SATURDAY

Again, follow the stickings to practice both right-hand and left-hand leads.

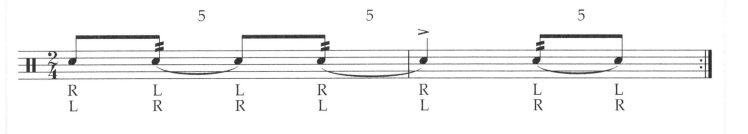

Here's one more Five Stroke Roll exercise.

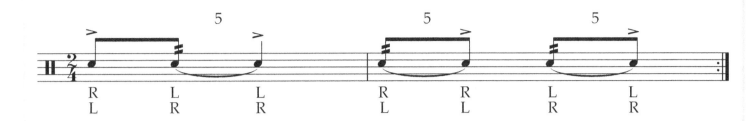

WEEK 12 SUMMARY EXERCISE

This week's challenge is to add musical dynamics to this 16-bar review exercise. Dynamics are varying degrees of volume. Use stick height to assist your volume production. *Forte* (*f*) is loud; *piano (p)* is soft.

WEEK 13: NINE & TEN STROKE ROLLS

MONDAY 85

Here's a preparatory exercise for the Nine Stroke Roll.

TUESDAY 86

Today, we'll phrase the Nine Stroke Roll as 16th notes.

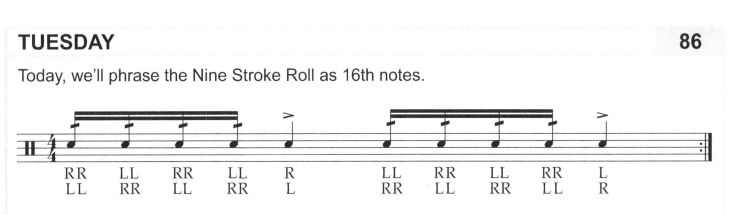

WEDNESDAY 87

This full-notation example utilizes a tie to phrase the Nine Stroke Roll.

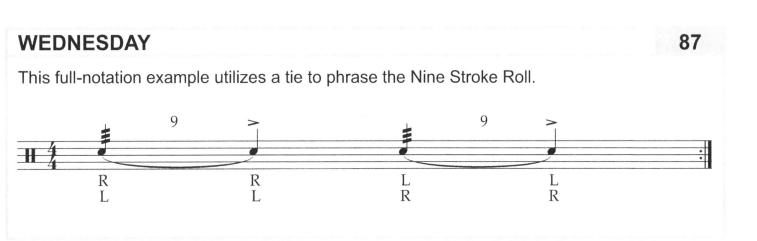

THURSDAY

Today's exercise phrases the Nine Stroke Roll on the "and" of beats 1 and 3.

FRIDAY

Count it, count it, count it out loud!

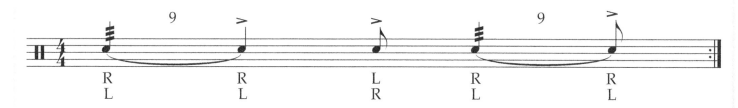

SATURDAY

Today, we'll try the Ten Stroke Roll. It's simple—you'll just add a single 16th note to the end of the Nine Stroke Roll.

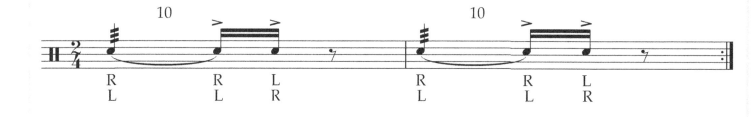

Today, we'll phrase the Ten Stroke roll on the "e" of beat 1 (bar 1) and the "and" of beat 1 (bar 2). Don't let the syncopation scare you; it's the same figure, just starting and ending in a different place within the pulse.

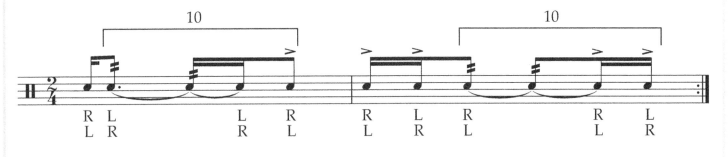

WEEK 13 SUMMARY EXERCISE

A *crescendo* marking (see bars 14–15) indicates that the music should get gradually louder. In this case, it starts as *piano* in bar 13 and finishes as *forte* in bar 16. Watch your counting in measure 15, where the phrase ends on the "e" of beat 2. Count while playing these rolls and play with a metronome!

WEEK 14: EIGHTH-NOTE TRIPLETS

MONDAY

Today, we introduce eighth-note triplets. Count aloud "1-o-let, 2-o-let, 3-o-let, 4-o-let."

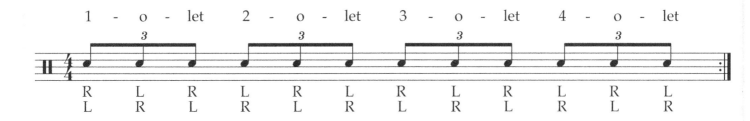

TUESDAY

Play all the accents in this exercise.

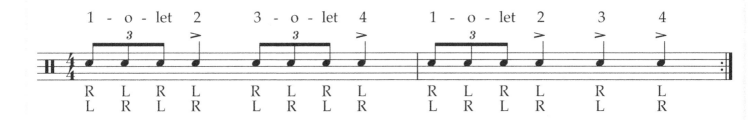

WEDNESDAY

Keep going with the counting!

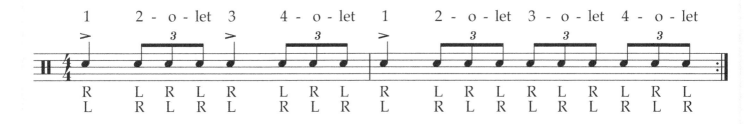

Here's another pattern that should be performed with accents.

This is a good time to use the metronome. Are you catching the difference in the groups of 2 and groups of 3 eighth notes?

This exercise features 3/4 time and some two-, three-, and four-note phrasing! Get that feel!

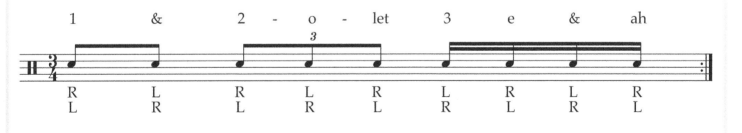

Be cautious with all the note subdivisions here. A metronome will be a good check on your rhythm.

WEEK 14 SUMMARY EXERCISE

This 16-bar exercise contains variations from this week's exercises, as well as a few new variations. Make sure to practice this summary exercise with a metronome.

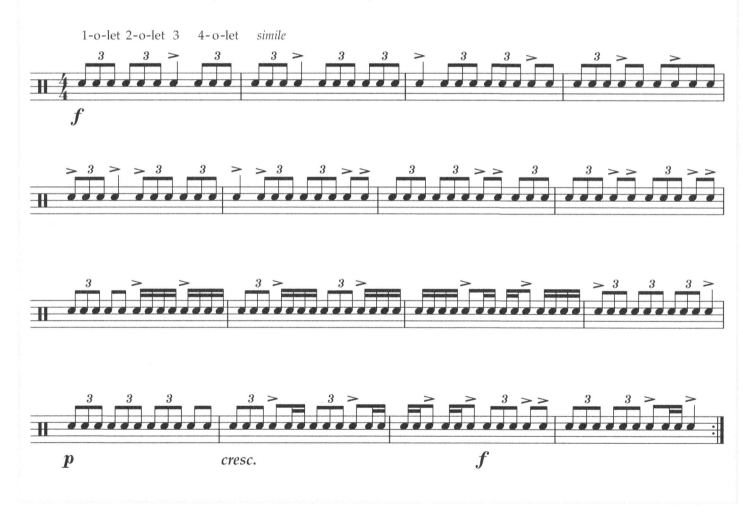

WEEK 15: THE FLAM TAP & FLAM ACCENT

MONDAY

Today's exercise introduces the Flam Tap.

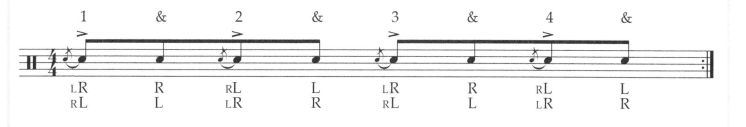

TUESDAY

Today, we work on the Flam Accent.

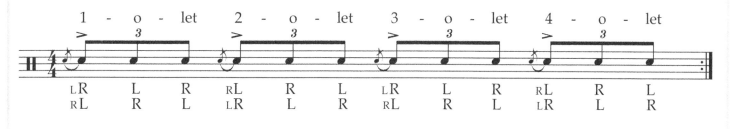

WEDNESDAY

Here's a rhythmic variation of the Flam Accent.

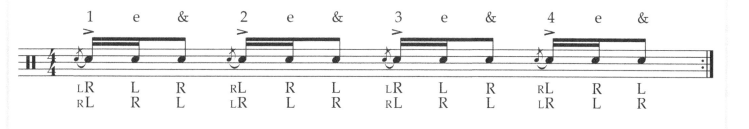

THURSDAY

Here's another rhythmic variation of the Flam Accent.

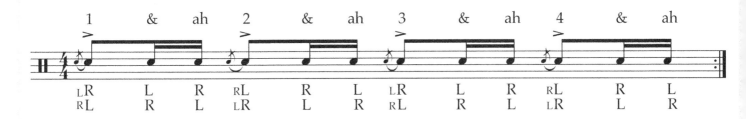

FRIDAY

Although tricky at first, this exercise will assist your accent-with-the-flam development.

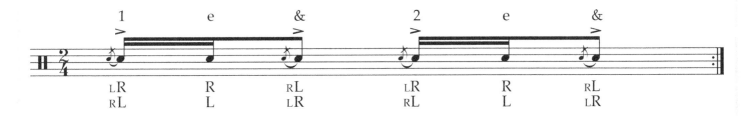

SATURDAY

You'll see Flam Taps in 16th notes in a lot of rudimental literature. Get to know them!

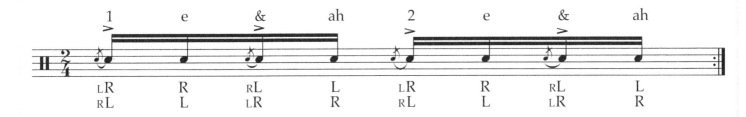

Here are some fun Flam Accents in a 16th-note pulse.

WEEK 15 SUMMARY EXERCISE

This week's review features Flam Accents and some new dynamic markings. *Mezzo piano* (*mp*) means moderately soft; *mezzo forte* (*mf*) means moderately loud.

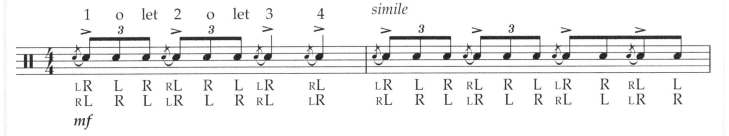

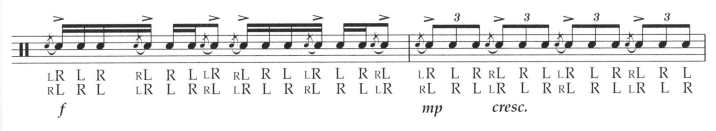

WEEK 16: FLAM PARADIDDLE & FLAMACUE

MONDAY

This week, we're going to get into some more Flam rudiments. Here's the Flam Paradiddle in eighth notes.

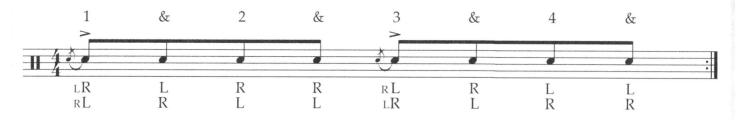

TUESDAY

Here's a primer for the Flamacue.

WEDNESDAY

Today, we're going to do some more Flamacue prep.

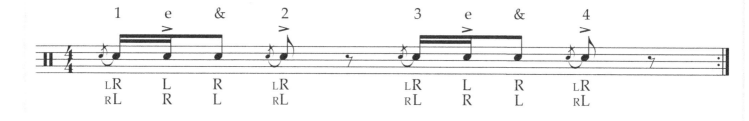

THURSDAY

Here's the Flamacue.

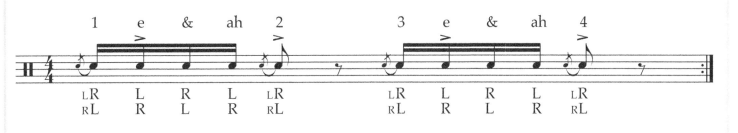

FRIDAY

Here's the Flam Paradiddle.

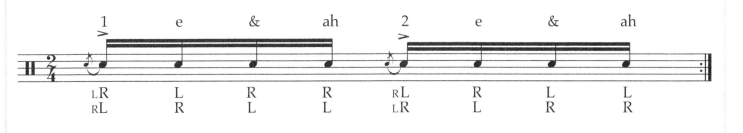

SATURDAY

Here's the Flam Paradiddle and The Flamacue.

Today, we have the Flamacue, followed by the Flam Paradiddle.

WEEK 16 SUMMARY EXERCISE

Here's another exercise utilizing dynamics. Very soft is *pianissimo* (*pp*); very loud is *fortissimo* (*ff*).

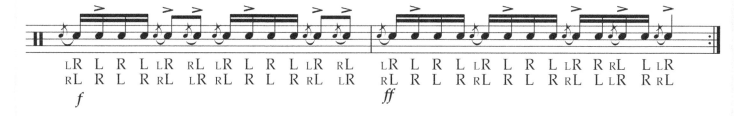

WEEK 17: 16TH-NOTE REVIEW

MONDAY 113

Make sure to count this syncopation.

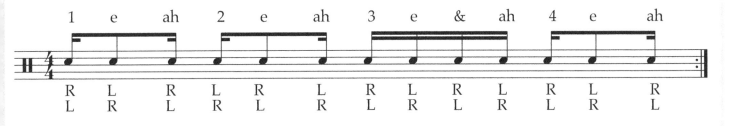

TUESDAY 114

We have lots of syncopation this week. Keep that counting habit alive and well.

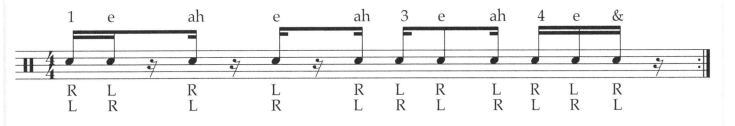

WEDNESDAY 115

Count out *all* the rests here!

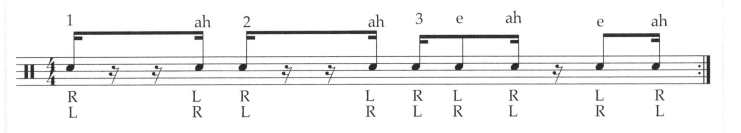

Watch out for those downbeat rests!

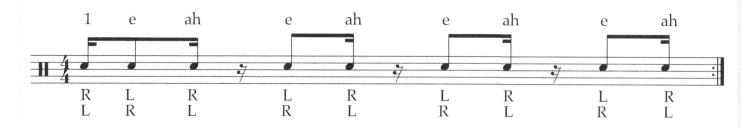

More syncopation. Count it!

Here we have The Paraddidle Diddle. Practice the repeats with the right-hand lead. When comfortable try the left-hand lead.

Space is the place… and lots of syncopations!

WEEK 17 SUMMARY EXERCISE

Counting is a must in this eight-bar exercise. Don't even think about being lazy. You've got to say it to play it!

MONDAY
120

Today, we play "false" sextuplets—a set of 16th-note triplets on each beat.

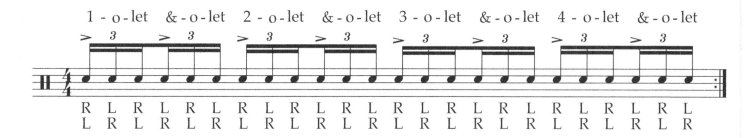

TUESDAY
121

Beats 1–3 feature a 16th-note triplet/eighth note grouping.

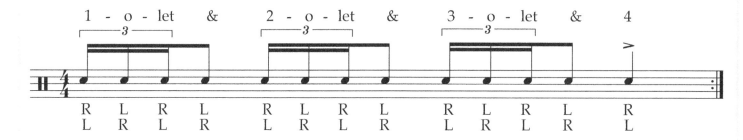

WEDNESDAY
122

Here's the inverse of yesterday's exercise. Now the eighth note precedes the 16th-note triplet.

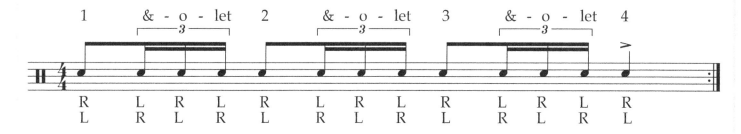

THURSDAY

Now the 16th-note triplet is followed by two 16th notes.

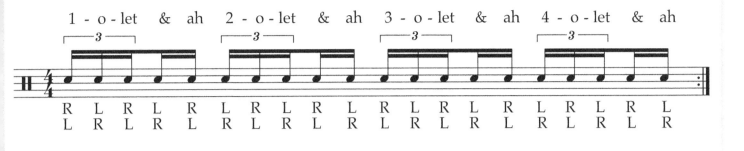

FRIDAY

Here's the inverse of yesterday's rhythm.

SATURDAY

Here's a combination of this week's rhythms.

Now we'll play "true" sextuplets. Accent the downbeat while feeling one set of six 16th notes.

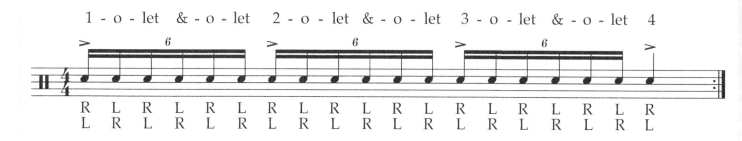

WEEK 18 SUMMARY EXERCISE

Lots of triplet subdivisions here. Your first attempt at this exercise might be rough, but you'll get it soon enough! Make sure to play along with your metronome and keep counting! You got this!

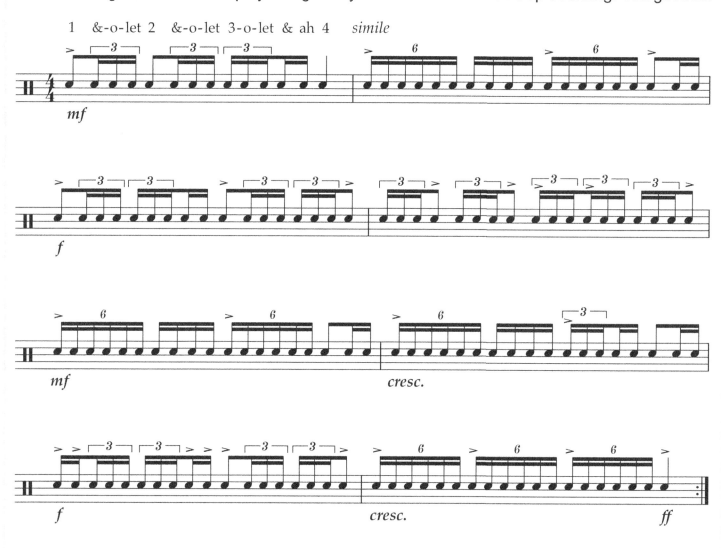

MONDAY 127

Today, we prep for the Seven Stroke Roll.

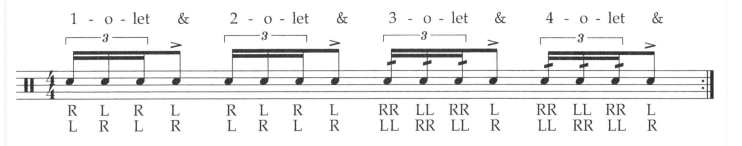

TUESDAY 128

Feel the pulse of the triplet as you perform the Seven Stroke Roll. You'll have four hand movements here: three Double Strokes and a final Single Stroke.

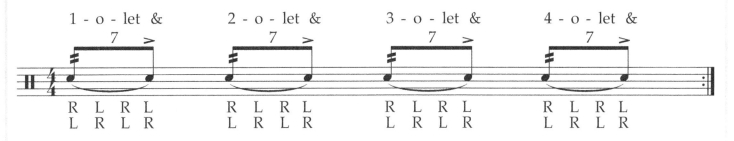

WEDNESDAY 129

Here's some Seven Stroke Roll prep on the "and" of the beat.

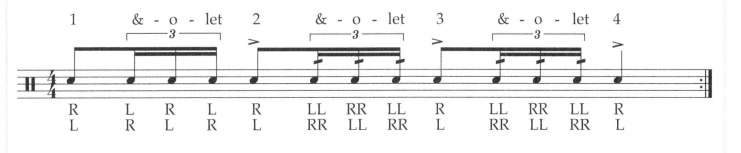

THURSDAY   130

Here, the Seven Stroke Roll occurs on the "and" of beats 1–3.

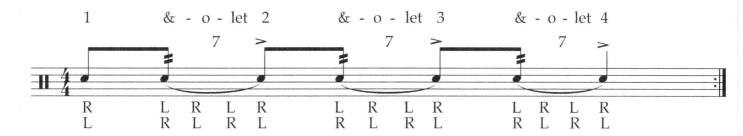

FRIDAY   131

Here, we have both downbeat and upbeat Seven Stroke Rolls.

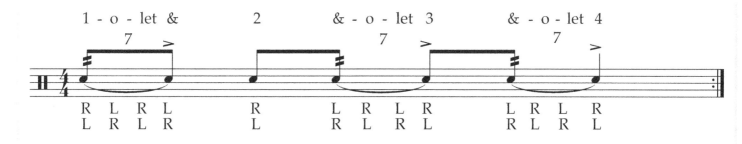

SATURDAY   132

This exercise features Seven Stroke Rolls with Flams.

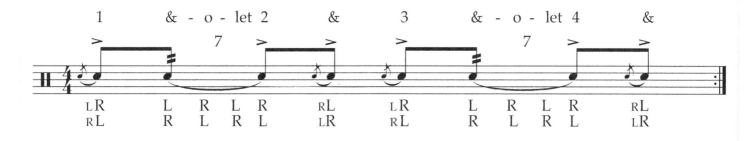

Here's another exercise with flams. Make sure that you're playing the rolls and flams cleanly.

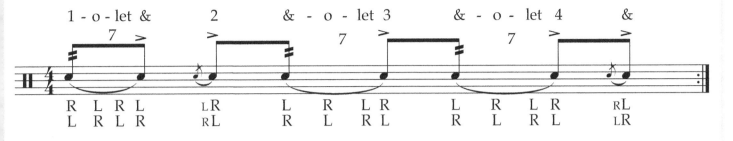

WEEK 19 SUMMARY EXERCISE

Have fun with this eight-bar exercise, which utilizes 16th-note triplets and the Seven Stroke Roll.

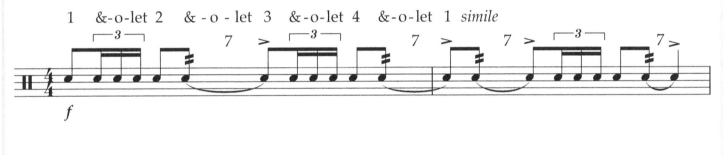

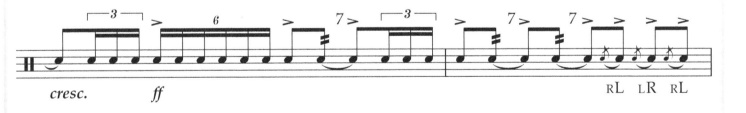

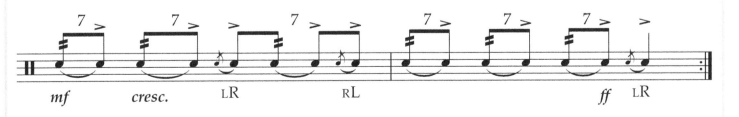

WEEK 20: THIRTEEN STROKE ROLL

MONDAY

Here's a preparatory exercise for the Thirteen Stroke Roll.

TUESDAY

Here's a preparatory exercise for the Thirteen Stoke Roll on the "and" of the beat.

WEDNESDAY

Today, we have the fully notated Thirteen Stroke Roll.

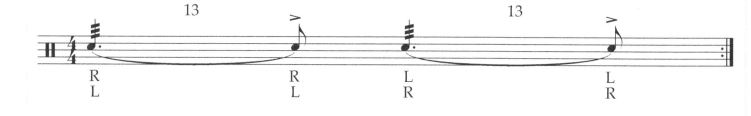

THURSDAY

Here's the Thirteen Stroke Roll on the "and" of the beat.

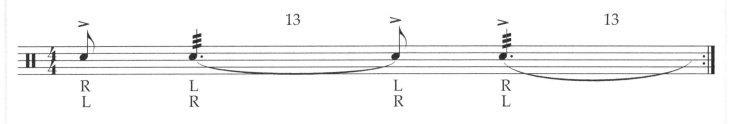

FRIDAY

Now, we're going to feel the Thirteen Stroke Roll in triplets.

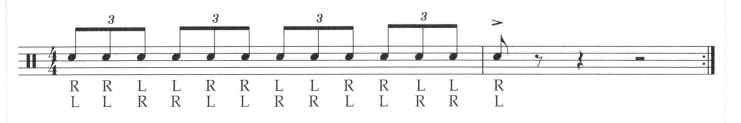

SATURDAY

Here's a quicker version of yesterday's exercise.

SUNDAY

Today's exercise combines the Five Stroke Roll and Thirteen Stroke Roll.

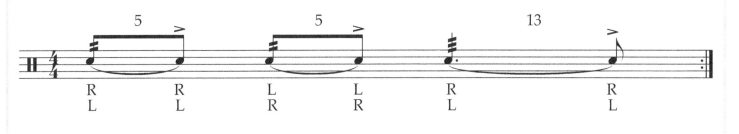

WEEK 20 SUMMARY EXERCISE

This week's summary exercise introduces the *marcato*. When you see the marcato symbol (^), play the note with sudden force and emphasis (slightly louder than an accent with a staccato-type note approach).

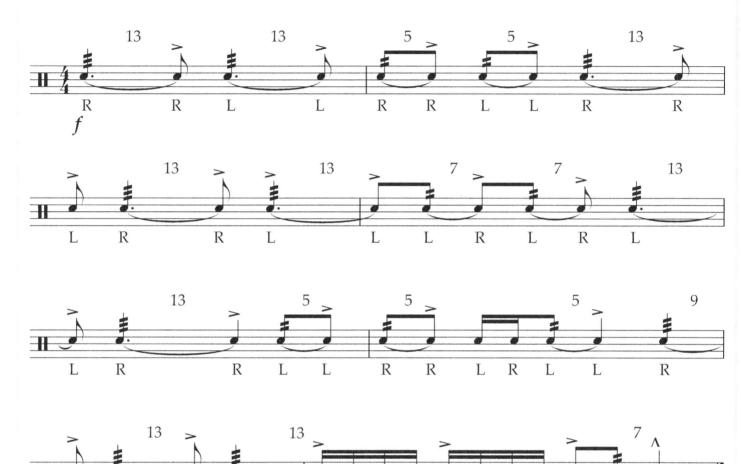

MONDAY   141

Here's a preparatory exercise for the Fifteen Stroke Roll.

TUESDAY   142

Today, we have the fully notated Fifteen Stroke Roll. Notice that you'll end the roll with the hand opposite to the one you start with.

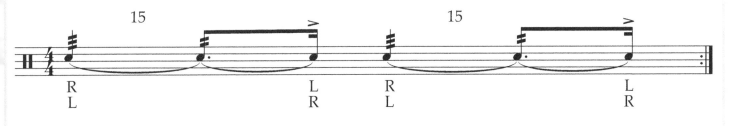

WEDNESDAY   143

Here's a preparatory exercise for the Fifteen Stroke Roll on the "and" of the beat.

THURSDAY 144

Here's the Fifteen Stroke Roll fully notated on the "e" of the beat.

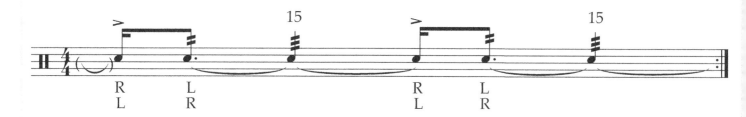

FRIDAY 145

Here's a preparatory exercise for the Seventeen Stroke Roll.

SATURDAY 146

Today, we have a fully notated Seventeen Stroke Roll in 3/4 time.

SUNDAY 147

This exercise combines the Seventeen Stroke Roll and Fifteen Stroke Roll.

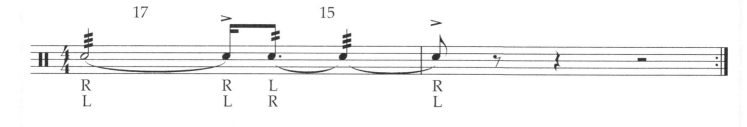

WEEK 21 SUMMARY EXERCISE

Lots of rolling! Lots of counting! The sound of the roll should be consistent, even, and balanced. Notice the "sfz" marking on beat 1 of the exercise. This is a *sforzando* marking, which means to play with a sudden and heavy accent.

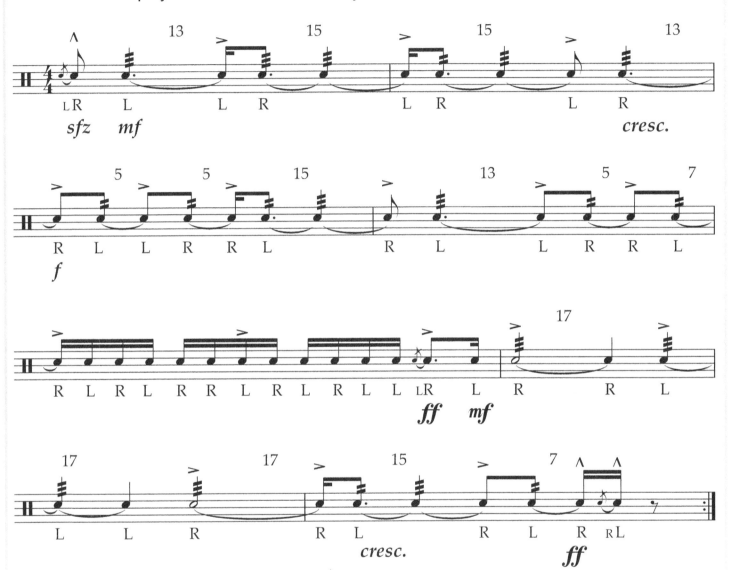

MONDAY   148

Today's exercise combines the Flam, Seven Stroke Roll, and Single Stroke Four.

TUESDAY   149

This exercise features the Flam, Five Stroke Roll, and Paradiddle-Diddle.

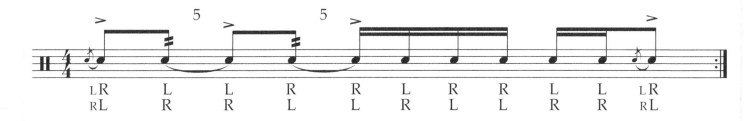

WEDNESDAY   150

Here's the Flam, Thirteen Stroke Roll, Five Stroke Roll, and Single Paradiddle in a single exercise.

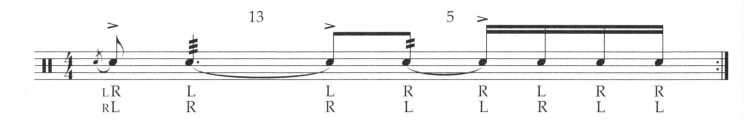

THURSDAY

Today, we have the Flam, Fifteen Stroke Roll, Seven Stroke Roll, and Single Paradiddle.

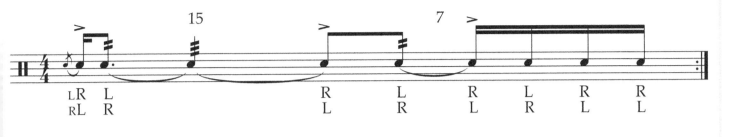

FRIDAY

This exercise features the Flam Paradiddle, the Flam, and the Ten Stroke Roll.

SATURDAY

Today, we have the Flam Tap and the Flam Paradiddle.

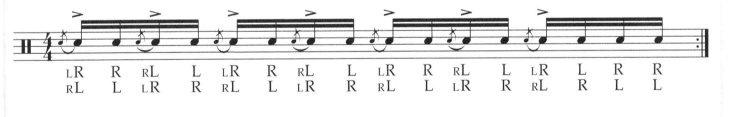

Here's the Flam Accent, Flam Paradiddle, and Flamacue.

WEEK 22 SUMMARY EXERCISE

Break out the metronome and start at 60 BPM, then increase your tempo by 10 clicks each time until you get the exercise up to a moderate tempo. Play your flams and rolls evenly—and play all the stickings! Have fun!

MONDAY
155

This week, we'll be experimenting with sounds on the snare drum. The first exercise involves playing from the edge of the drum to the center. Experiment with all kinds of rhythm but try to play your Concert Roll from the top edge to the center. Then try it as a Double Stroke Open Roll. Notice the different tones, as well as the increase in volume when reaching the center of the head.

TUESDAY
156

Next, we'll experiment with stick shots. Place one stick onto the head and strike the stick at or after the shoulder with the other stick.

WEDNESDAY
157

Next, we'll try a rimshot. Play your stick so that the shoulder of the stick strikes the rim and head simultaneously. This will produce a loud "crack" sound.

THURSDAY

Today, we're going to spotlight the tenor drum. Turn off your snare throw to disengage the wires. *Voilà*—you have the tenor drum sound! Use this sound and experiment with your playing.

FRIDAY

Now use the rimshot and stick shot on the tenor drum.

SATURDAY

Today, you'll practice playing on the snare drum rim (counterhoop), at the top of the drum, with the neck of your sticks. This technique produces a lighter, "woody" sound.

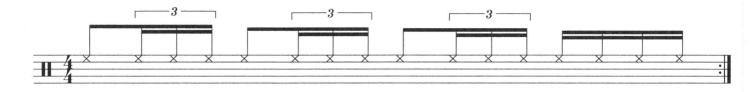

SUNDAY

Play these Single Stroke Fours and Sevens between the rim and center of the drum.

WEEK 23 SUMMARY EXERCISE

This exercise will provide you with a summary of sounds that you can produce on your snare drum. Perform it very slowly at first!

WEEK 24: SINGLE & DOUBLE RATAMACUE

MONDAY

162

Here's a Single Ratamacue preparatory exercise. Play two grace notes before the triplet.

TUESDAY

163

Here's the traditional notation of the Single Ratamacue.

WEDNESDAY

164

Here's a preparatory exercise for the Single Ratamacue on the downbeat.

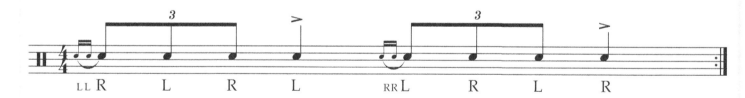

THURSDAY

165

Say "Rat-a-ma-cue." It's an onomatopoeia!

FRIDAY

Make sure to perform the accents here!

SATURDAY

Here's the Double Ratamacue. Play two Drags of the same sticking before the triplet.

SUNDAY

Play this exercise slowly at first. The accents are important.

WEEK 24 SUMMARY EXERCISE

Notice the first and second endings on the first four-bar phrase. Take the first ending only once, then move to the second ending for the eighth measure of the first half of the exercise. Play *forte* the first time through, then play *fortissimo* the second time. Be cautious of the 16th-note rests in the last line of the exercise.

WEEK 25: SINGLE STROKE FOUR & MORE

MONDAY

We've played this rhythm before but now let's identify it as a rudiment: the Single Stroke Four.

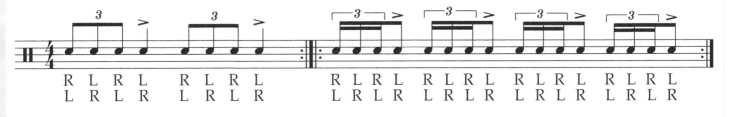

TUESDAY

Here's the Four Stroke Ruff. Play three alternating taps before the main note.

WEDNESDAY

Today, we'll practice alternative stickings for the Four Stroke Ruff.

THURSDAY

Here are even more alternative stickings for the Four Stroke Ruff.

FRIDAY

We've played this rhythm before but now let's identify it as a rudiment: the Single Stroke Seven.

SATURDAY

Today's exercise is a combination of the Single Stoke Four, Four Stroke Ruff, and Single Stroke Seven.

SUNDAY

Play the accent at the end of the Single Stroke Seven.

WEEK 25 SUMMARY EXERCISE

Triplets, triplets, triplets! Play evenly and perform with dynamics and accents.

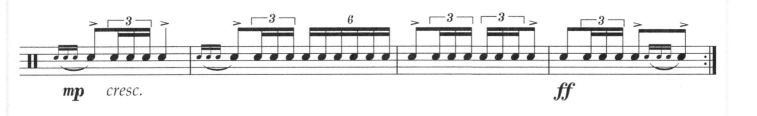

WEEK 26: SINGLE DRAG TAP

MONDAY

We'll start this week with a preparatory exercise for the Single Drag Tap.

TUESDAY

Here's the traditional notation of the Single Drag Tap.

WEDNESDAY

This exercise syncopates the Single Drag Tap.

THURSDAY

Here's another Single Drag Tap example with multiple syncopations.

Today, we'll add a drag to the Single Stroke Seven.

This exercise features Single Drag Taps with doubles on the measured beat pulse instead of a grace note. This is often seen in contemporary rudimental solos and in modern marching arrangements.

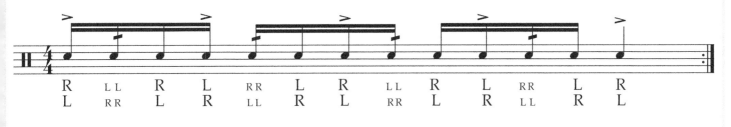

Back to traditional phrasing, play the drag into the rhythm.

WEEK 26 SUMMARY EXERCISE

Here is a summary exercise that falls into the category of Traditional Rudimental Snare Drum soloing. Play the accents, as well as clean grace notes before the beat. You'll get the feel of it with time and practice.

WEEK 27: THE LESSON 25

MONDAY

Here's a preparatory exercise for The Lesson 25 rudiment. This rudiment gets its name from the 25th lesson in the book *Strube's Drum and Fife Instructor* (1869) by Gardiner A. Strube.

TUESDAY

Here's the traditional notation of The Lesson 25 rudiment.

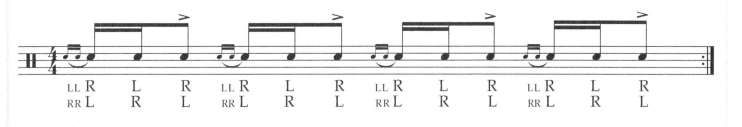

WEDNESDAY

This exercise is an inversion of The Lesson 25 rudiment.

THURSDAY

Follow the stickings in this Lesson 25 combination exercise.

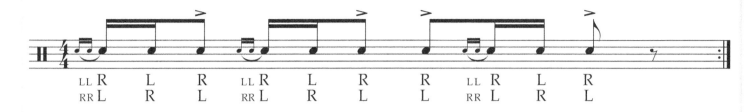

FRIDAY

Here's a combination of The Lesson 25 and Single Ratamacue rudiments.

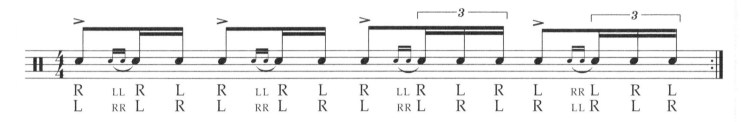

SATURDAY

This exercise inverts The Lesson 25 and Single Ratamacue rudiments from yesterday.

SUNDAY

Today, we'll combine the Single Ratamacue, Lesson 25, and Single Drag Tap rudiments.

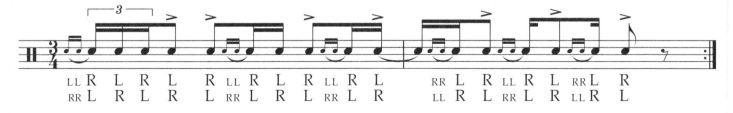

WEEK 27 SUMMARY EXERCISE

This summary is another exercise in the style of Traditional Rudimental Drumming. Pay close attention to the stickings, accents, and dynamics.

WEEK 28: THE LESSON 25 VARIATIONS

MONDAY   190

Today, we'll look at The Lesson 25 when notated "on the beat" and to be played at fast tempi in contemporary and modern drumming.

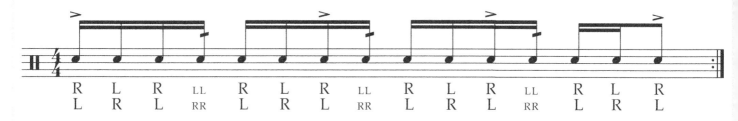

TUESDAY   191

Here's The Lesson 25 inversion when notated "on the beat" and to be played at fast tempi.

WEDNESDAY   192

This variation is referred to as the "Berger 25," so named after the Swiss drumming icon Dr. Fritz Berger, as referenced in his drum solo "Rudimenter Good Luck" (Basle-America Mixpickles) from *America's N.A.R.D. Drum Solos* (Ludwig Music Publishing).

THURSDAY

Here, we combine The Lesson 25 and Berger 25.

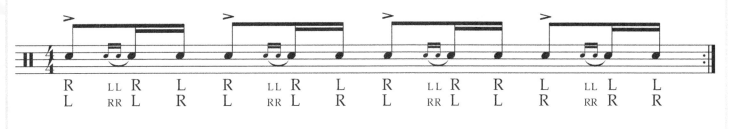

FRIDAY

Here are Lesson 25s "on the beat" and to be played at fast tempi.

SATURDAY

Today's exercise combines the Berger 25 and Single Ratamacue.

SUNDAY

Here are more Lesson 25s "on the beat."

WEEK 28 SUMMARY EXERCISE

This week's summary exercise features some traditional rudiments and a section of contemporary playing at a faster tempo. Be patient if you can't play all this music right away; just keep working on it, and, in time, you'll get it!

Moderate march tempo

FASTER!

88

MONDAY 197

We start this week with a preparatory exercise for the Triple Ratamacue. Play three Drags before the triplet.

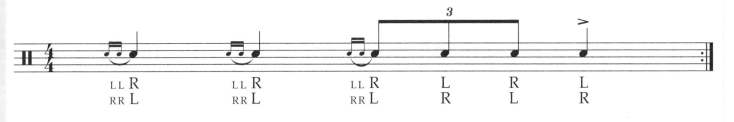

TUESDAY 198

Here's the Triple Ratamacue as traditionally notated.

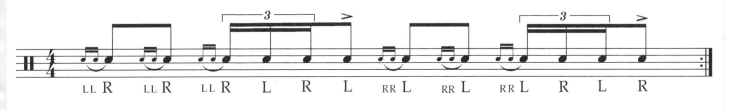

WEDNESDAY 199

Here's a mix of the Single Ratamacue and Triple Ratamacue.

THURSDAY

Today, we'll combine The Lesson 25, the Drag, and the Triple Ratamacue.

FRIDAY

Now let's mix the Triple Ratamacue, The Lesson 25, and the Five Stroke Roll.

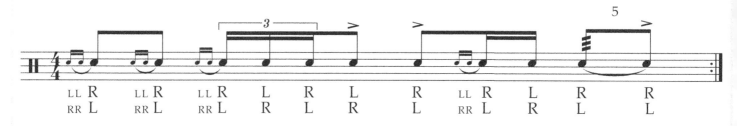

SATURDAY

Here, we combine the Double Ratamacue, the Drag, and the Triple Ratamacue.

SUNDAY

We'll end this week with a combination of the Drag, Single Stroke Four, and Triple Ratamacue.

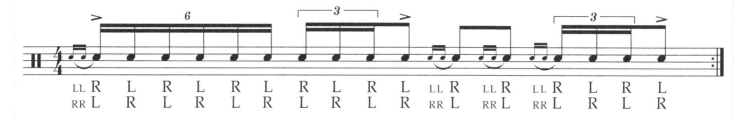

WEEK 29 SUMMARY EXERCISE

Watch your stickings, form, and dynamics while playing this traditional rudimental exercise.

WEEK 30: DRAG PARADIDDLE #1 & #2

MONDAY

Here's a preparatory exercise for the Drag Paradiddle #1.

TUESDAY

Here's the Drag Paradiddle #1 as traditionally notated.

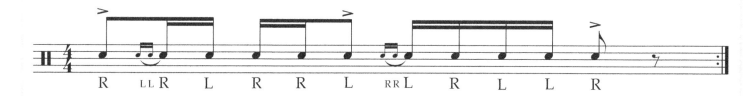

WEDNESDAY

Here's the Drag Paradiddle #1 with syncopated beaming.

THURSDAY

Now let's play a preparatory exercise for the Drag Paradiddle #2.

FRIDAY

Here's the Drag Paradiddle #2 as traditionally notated.

SATURDAY

209

Today, we're going to practice the inversion of the Drag Paradiddle #2.

SUNDAY

210

Today's exercise is a mix of the Drag Paradiddle #1 and the Drag Paradiddle #2.

WEEK 30 SUMMARY EXERCISE

For a musical experience, play all the stickings and dynamics. Always work up new music slowly. Keep playing this one—you'll get it!

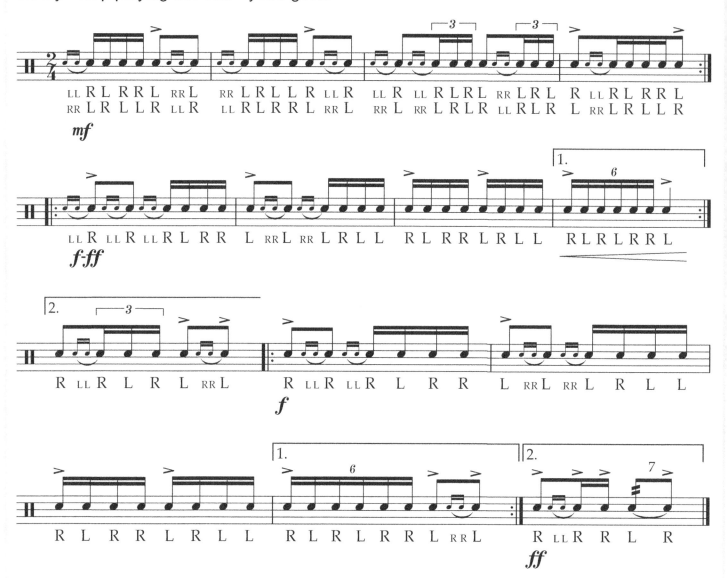

WEEK 31: COMPOUND METER – 6/8 TIME

MONDAY

This exercise is in 6/8 time, a compound meter. Count six eighth notes in each measure.

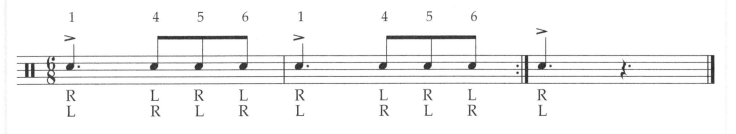

TUESDAY

Make sure to count the rests here!

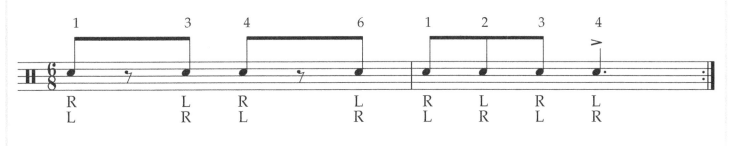

WEDNESDAY

For this exercise, count in 16th notes: "1-&, 2-&, 3-&, 4-&, 5-&, 6-&," etc.

THURSDAY

214

Make sure to count the rhythmic variations in this example.

FRIDAY

215

Watch out for the rests on the downbeats in this exercise.

SATURDAY

216

The 16th-note rests look challenging at first but just make sure to keep counting.

SUNDAY

217

Here are some really syncopated figures. If you have trouble with the phrasing, use a metronome.

WEEK 31 SUMMARY EXERCISE

Bust out that metronome and play! Count your rhythms and have fun!

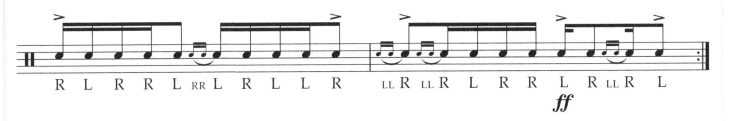

WEEK 32: DOUBLE DRAG TAP & MORE

MONDAY   218

Here's the Double Drag Tap in 6/8. Make sure to count the "and" on beat 2 and beat 5.

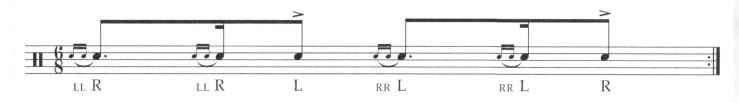

TUESDAY   219

This exercise is a mix of the Double Drag Tap and Drag Paradiddle #1.

WEDNESDAY   220

Today, we're going to invert yesterday's Double Drag Tap and Drag Paradiddle #1 exercise.

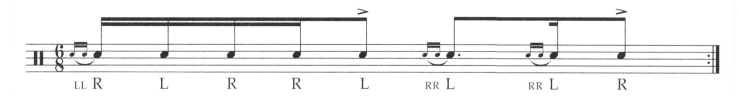

THURSDAY   221

Here's a mix of the Single Ratamacue and Double Drag Tap.

FRIDAY

Today, we're going to mix the Double Drag Tap and Double Ratamacue.

SATURDAY

Here's another exercise that mixes the Double Ratamacue and Double Drag Tap.

SUNDAY

We'll close out this week with a mix of Drag Paradiddle #2, the Single Ratamacue, and the Double Drag Tap.

WEEK 32 SUMMARY EXERCISE

Ready for rudiments? Of course, you are! Play the stickings and enjoy this exercise.

R ll R L R L rr L rr L R   ll R ll R L rr L R L R

f

ll R ll R L rr L rr L R L   ll R ll R L rr L rr L R L R

ll R ll R L R R L rr L R L L   R ll R L R R L rr L R L R

mf   *cresc.*

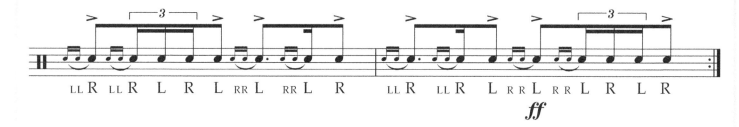

ll R ll R L R L rr L rr L R   ll R ll R L rr L rr L R L R

ff

WEEK 33: 10-WEEK REVIEW #3

MONDAY

We start this week with a mix of the Single Drag Tap and the Drag Paradiddle #2.

TUESDAY

Here's a mix of the Single Stroke Seven, The Lesson 25, and the Four Stroke Ruff.

WEDNESDAY

Today, we combine the Single Ratamacue, The Lesson 25, and the Single Stroke Four.

THURSDAY

Now, we'll mix the Single Stroke Four and a *true* sextuplet.

FRIDAY

229

This exercise is a combination of The Lesson 25, the Double Ratamacue, and the Single Stroke Four.

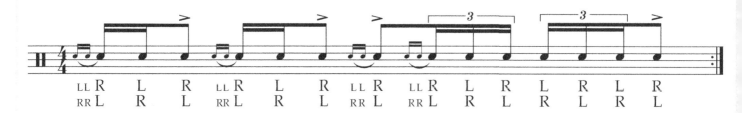

SATURDAY

230

Today, we're going to mix the Four Stroke Ruff and the Drag.

SUNDAY

231

Here, we combine the Drag Paradiddle #2, the Single Ratamacue, and The Lesson 25.

WEEK 33 SUMMARY EXERCISE

Make sure to catch all the repeats and dynamics in this exercise!

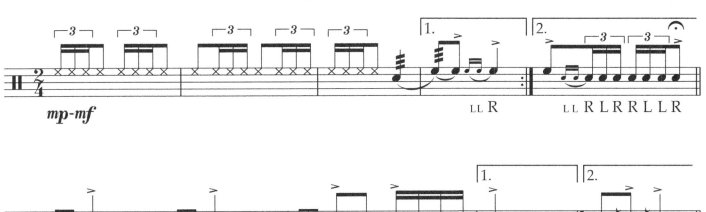

WEEK 34: 9/8 & 12/8 TIME SIGNATURES

MONDAY

Today, we're going to work on another compound time signature, 9/8. Now, we'll count *nine* eighth notes in each measure.

TUESDAY

233

Don't fret! Just count! You got this!

WEDNESDAY

234

Make sure to count and feel the upbeats in this exercise.

THURSDAY

235

Now it's time to practice some rudiments in 9/8.

FRIDAY

Today, we're going to work on yet another compound time signature, 12/8. Now, we'll count *twelve* eighth notes in each measure.

SATURDAY

If you have trouble feeling this measure as a whole, break it down into four groups of three eighth-note beats

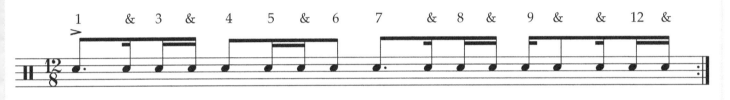

SUNDAY

Make sure to count this exercise so that you can feel the upbeats.

WEEK 34 SUMMARY EXERCISE

Make sure to count all the beats in each measure as you practice. Remember, you can break down this meter into smaller groups of three eighth notes if you find yourself struggling with the measures as a whole.

MONDAY 239

Let's start the week with a preparatory exercise for the Six Stroke Roll.

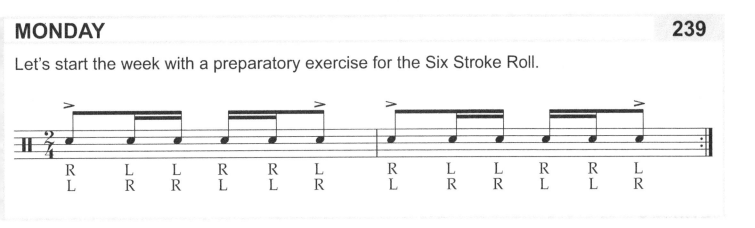

TUESDAY 240

Here's another preparatory exercise for the Six Stroke Roll.

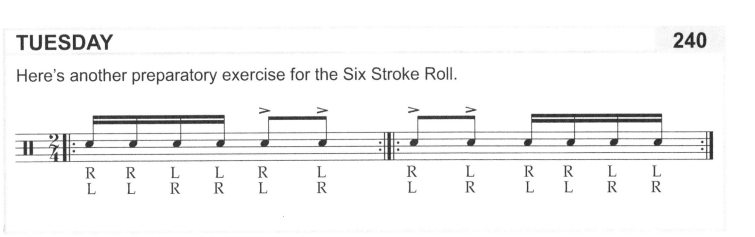

WEDNESDAY 241

Here's the Six Stroke Roll notated on the beat, just as you'd see in modern notation.

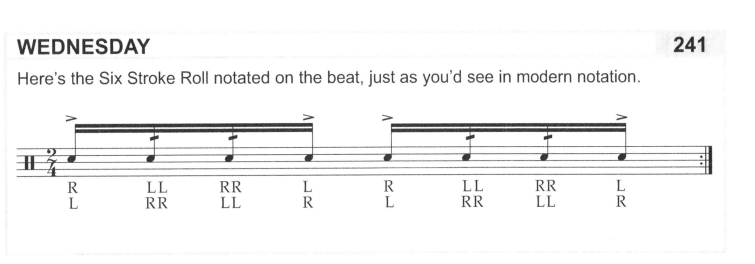

THURSDAY

This exercise is a variation of the Six Stroke Roll.

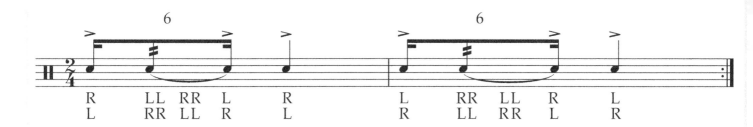

FRIDAY

Now let's try the Six Stroke Roll in a triplet feel.

SATURDAY

Today's focus is the Eleven Stroke Roll, starting with a preparatory exercise.

SUNDAY

Here's a variation of the Eleven Stroke Roll.

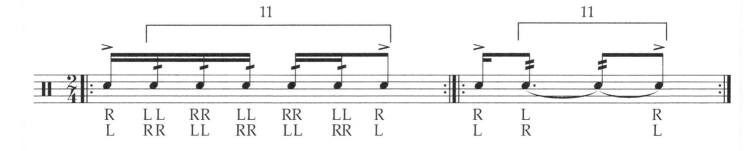

WEEK 35 SUMMARY EXERCISE

Counting is key to this roll summary exercise.

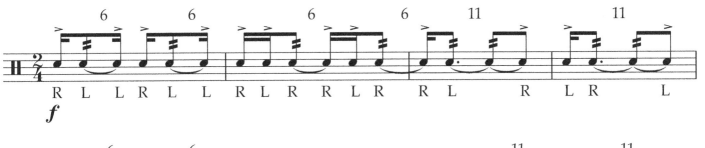

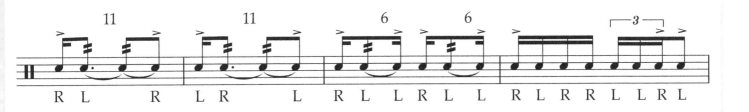

WEEK 36: SINGLE DRAGADIDDLE & MORE

MONDAY

We're going to start this week with a preparatory exercise for the Single Dragadiddle.

TUESDAY

Here's the Single Dragadiddle in full notation.

WEDNESDAY

Here's the Pataflafla, which is an onomatopoeia: "Pa-Ta-Fla(m)-Fla(m)".

THURSDAY

Now let's play the Pataflafla as a phrase.

FRIDAY

Today's exercise is a mix of the Single Dragadiddle and the Pataflafla.

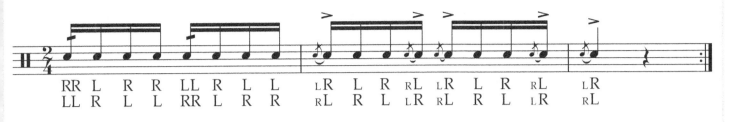

SATURDAY

Today, we're going to mix the Pataflafla with a variation of the Single Dragadiddle.

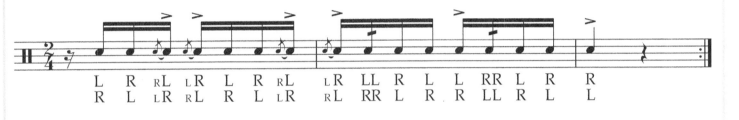

SUNDAY

This exercise combines Drag Paradiddle #2 and the Single Dragadiddle.

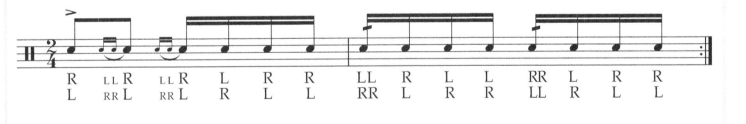

WEEK 36 SUMMARY EXERCISE

Play all of this very slowly. Don't worry—you'll get it! Enjoy the journey! If you don't get it all this week, just keep going! You can alway come back and practice this exercise at another time.

MONDAY

This week begins with a preparatory exercise for the Swiss Army Triplet.

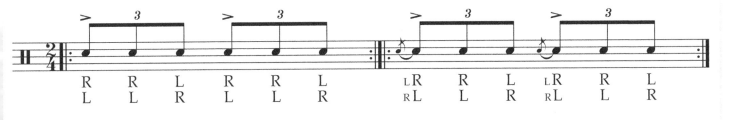

TUESDAY

Here's the Swiss Army Triplet in full notation.

WEDNESDAY

Today, we're going to work on a preparatory exercise for the Single Flammed Mill.

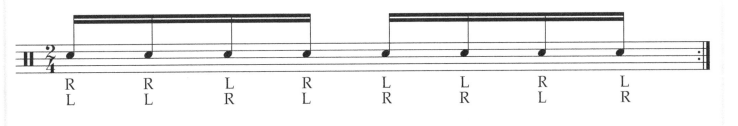

Here's the Single Flammed Mill in full notation.

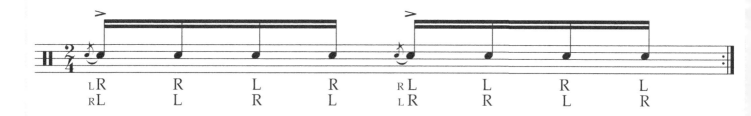

Today's exercise combines the Single Flammed Mill and the Pataflafla.

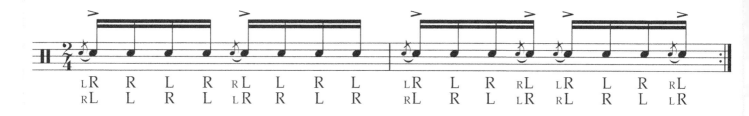

Today, we'll combine the Swiss Army Triplet with the Pataflafla.

Lots of rudiments in this exercise. Catch all the stickings!

WEEK 37 SUMMARY EXERCISE

Pay close attention to your stickings and use a metronome while performing this summary exercise.

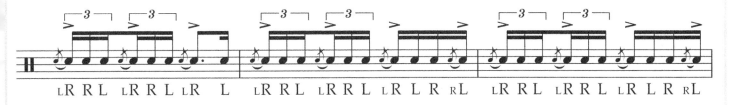

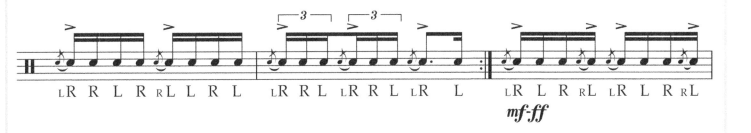

MONDAY

260

Our first asymmetrical meter is 5/4. Either count to 5 or in groups of 2 + 3.

TUESDAY

261

Again, either count to 5 or in groups of 2 + 3.

WEDNESDAY

262

As before, either count to 5 or in groups of 2 + 3.

THURSDAY

263

Here, either count to 5 or in groups of 3 + 2.

FRIDAY

Like yesterday, count to 5 or in groups of 3 + 2.

SATURDAY

How would you count this exercise?

SUNDAY

Try this 5/4 phrase with rudiments!

WEEK 38 SUMMARY EXERCISE

Whichever way you decide to count, just make sure to count!

MONDAY

Our next asymmetrical meter is 7/4. Either count to 7 or in groups of 2 + 2 + 3.

TUESDAY

Again, either count to 7 or in groups of 2 + 2 + 3.

WEDNESDAY

Now count to 7 or in groups of 2 + 3 + 2.

THURSDAY

Like yesterday, either count to 7 or in groups of 2 + 3 + 2.

FRIDAY

Here, you can either count to 7 or in groups of 3 + 2 + 2.

SATURDAY

Like yesterday, either count to 7 or in groups of 3 + 2 + 2.

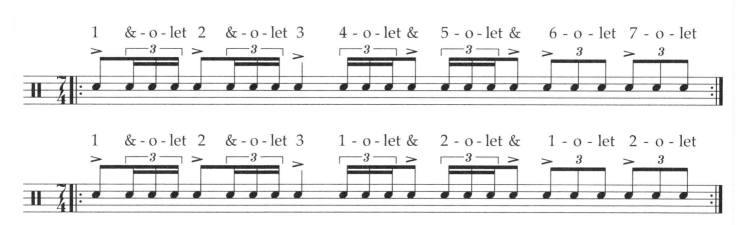

SUNDAY

What phrasing would you use here?

WEEK 39 SUMMARY EXERCISE

Whichever way you decide to count, just make sure to count!

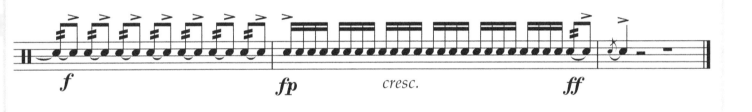

WEEK 40: FIVE & SIX STROKE RUFFS

MONDAY 274

We're going to start this week with a Five Stroke Ruff preparatory exercises.

TUESDAY 275

Here's the Five Stroke Ruff as traditionally notated.

WEDNESDAY 276

Today, we're going to work on a Six Stroke Ruff preparatory exercise. The five 16th notes are phrased as a quintuplet.

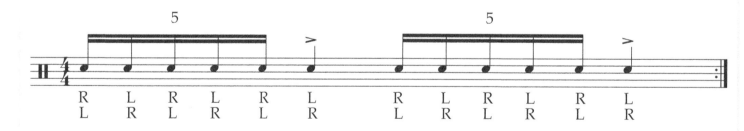

Here's the Six Stroke Ruff as traditionally notated.

Now, we're going to combine the Five Stroke and Six Stroke Ruffs.

Here's a Ruff combination.

We'll end this week with another Ruff combination.

WEEK 40 SUMMARY EXERCISE

Timing is everything when performing these patterns. Make sure to stay relaxed and play light taps before the main notes of the Ruffs.

WEEK 41: ASYMMETRICAL TIME – 5/8 METER

MONDAY
281

Our next asymmetrical meter is 5/8. Either count to 5 or in groups of 2 + 3.

TUESDAY
282

Again, either count to 5 or in groups of 2 + 3.

WEDNESDAY
283

As before, either count to 5 or in groups of 2 + 3.

THURSDAY
284

Here, you can count to 5 or in groups of 3 + 2.

FRIDAY

Like yesterday, count to 5 or in groups of 3 + 2.

SATURDAY

Don't forget to use a metronome to assist in counting the exercise.

SUNDAY

Make sure to keep counting!

WEEK 41 SUMMARY EXERCISE

Whichever way you decide to count, just make sure to count!

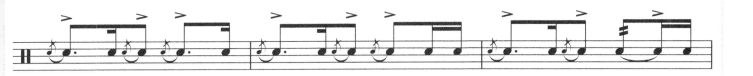

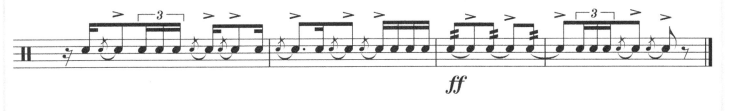

WEEK 42: ASYMMETRICAL TIME – 7/8 METER

MONDAY

Our final asymmetrical meter is 7/8. Either count to 7 or in groups of 2 + 2 + 3.

TUESDAY

Again, either count to 7 or in groups of 2 + 2 + 3.

WEDNESDAY

Here, you can either count to 7 or in groups of 2 + 3 + 2.

THURSDAY

Like yesterday, either count to 7 or in groups of 2 + 3 + 2.

FRIDAY

For this exercise, either count to 7 or in groups of 3 + 2 + 2.

SATURDAY

Like yesterday, either count to 7 or in groups of 3 + 2 + 2.

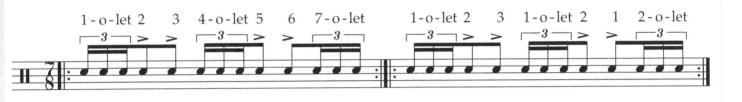

SUNDAY

Here's a fun two-measure phrase in 7/8. Make sure to count! Note that, as your tempo increases in this exercise, the roll phrasing will also change.

WEEK 42 SUMMARY EXERCISE

Whichever way you decide to count, just make sure to count!

MONDAY 295

This exercise combines Six Stroke and Eleven Stroke Rolls.

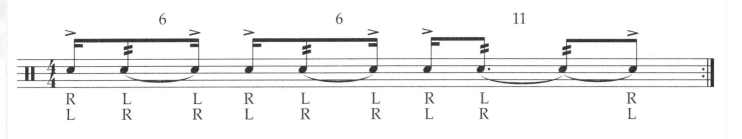

TUESDAY 296

Today, we're going to mix the Single Dragadiddle and the Pataflafla.

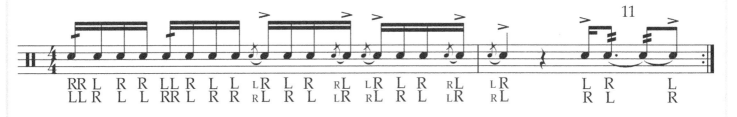

WEDNESDAY 297

Today's exercise features a mix of the Swiss Army Triplet and the Single Flammed Mill.

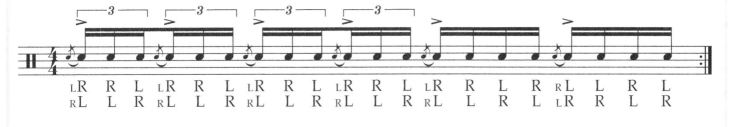

THURSDAY

Here, we combine the Five Stroke and Six Stroke Ruffs.

FRIDAY

Todays' exercise is a review of 9/8 meter.

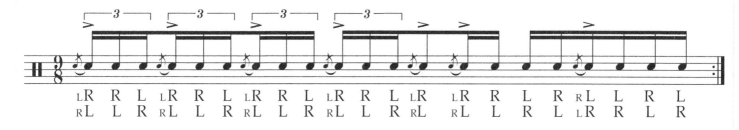

SATURDAY

Todays' exercise is a review of 12/8 meter.

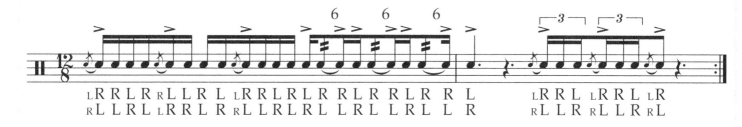

SUNDAY

Todays' exercise is a review of 7/8 meter.

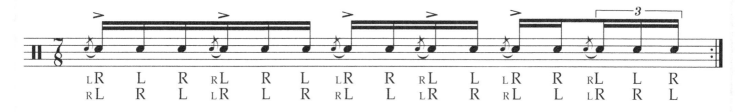

WEEK 43 SUMMARY EXERCISE

Practice, practice, practice! You've come a long way. Keep up the good work!

WEEK 44: FLAM DRAG & MORE

MONDAY

This week starts with a Flam Drag preparatory exercise.

TUESDAY

Here's the Flam Drag in full notation.

WEDNESDAY

Today, we're going to perform the Flam Drag in 6/8 time.

THURSDAY

Now let's play the Flam Drag as triplets.

FRIDAY

Here's a preparatory exercise to introduce you to the Flam Paradiddle-Diddle.

SATURDAY

Here's the Flam Paradiddle-Diddle in full notation.

SUNDAY

This exercise combines Flam Drag Triplets and the Flam Paradiddle-Diddle.

WEEK 44 SUMMARY EXERCISE

Lots of rudiments here! As your rudiment playing improves, you'll still need to continue practicing them. Make sure all flams and rolls are sharp and tight. Have fun!

WEEK 45: INVERTED FLAM TAP

MONDAY

We start this week with a preparatory exercise for the Inverted Flam Tap.

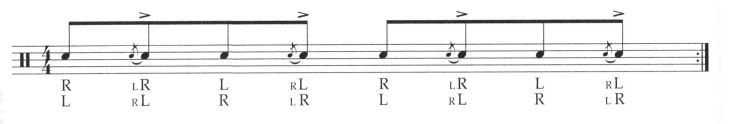

TUESDAY

Here's the Inverted Flam Tap in full notation.

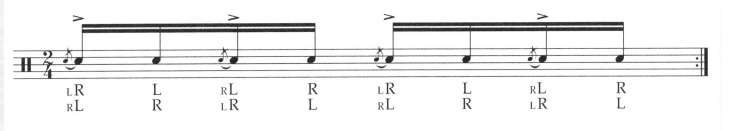

WEDNESDAY

Today, we combine the Inverted Flam Tap and the Pataflafla.

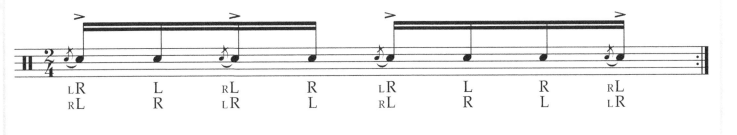

THURSDAY

This exercise is a mix of the Flamacue and Inverted Flam Tap.

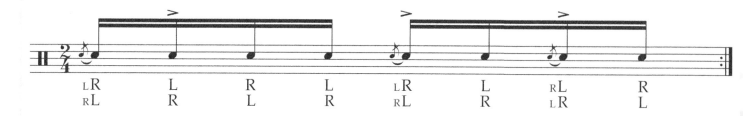

FRIDAY

Here's a longer phrase featuring the Flam Accent. Invert your sticking on the repeat.

SATURDAY

This phrase is a mix of the Pataflafla and Inverted Flam Tap.

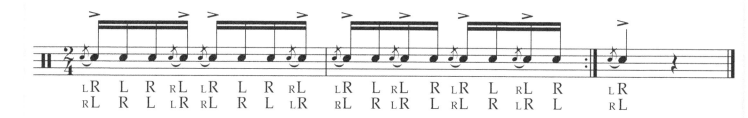

SUNDAY

Today's exercise combines the Inverted Flam Tap and Flam Paradiddle-Diddle.

WEEK 45 SUMMARY EXERCISE

Here we go! Another rudimental summary! You're developing some major skills. Keep up the great work!

WEEK 46: MIXED TIME SIGNATURES

MONDAY

This mixed-meter exercise combines a measure of 3/4 and a measure of 5/4. Make sure to use a metronome to help with counting!

TUESDAY

This mixed-meter exercise combines a measure of 4/4 and a measure of 3/4.

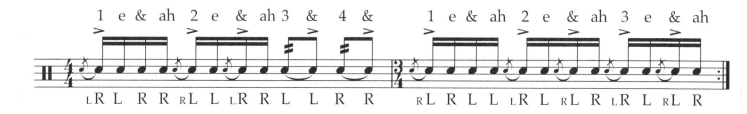

WEDNESDAY

Today, we have another mixed-meter exercise, this time combining 5/8 and 7/8 time signatures.

THURSDAY

Here's another mixed-meter example. Today, we combine 7/8 and 9/8 meters.

FRIDAY

This mixed-meter exercise combines *three* meters: 7/8, 5/8, and 9/8.

SATURDAY

Similar to yesterday's mixed-meter example, this exercise features a measure of 5/8, 7/8, and 3/4. Make sure to set your metronome and keep counting the eighth note.

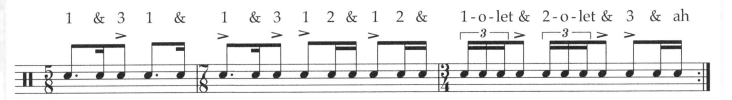

SUNDAY

Now let's add some rudiments to a mixed-meter exercise. Make sure to count this three-meter (5/8, 7/8, and 3/4) example!

WEEK 46 SUMMARY EXERCISE

We wrap up this week with a mixed-meter summary exercise. Make sure to turn on your metronome and count!

142

MONDAY 323

This week, we review the Single Stroke Roll, Single Stroke Four, Single Stroke Seven, and Triple Stroke Roll. Here's an exercise to work on your Single Stroke Roll.

TUESDAY 324

Here's a review of the Single Stroke Roll.

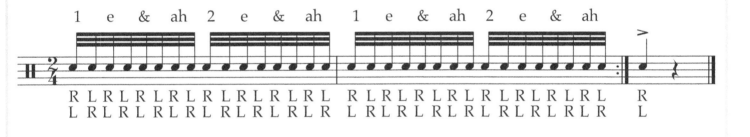

WEDNESDAY 325

Here's a review of the Single Stroke Seven and Single Stroke of Four.

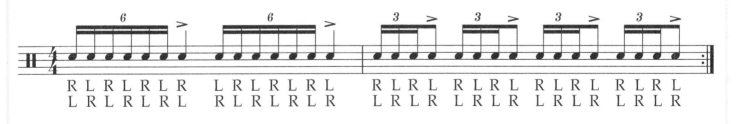

THURSDAY

Today, we're going to review the Single Stroke Seven and Triple Stroke Roll.

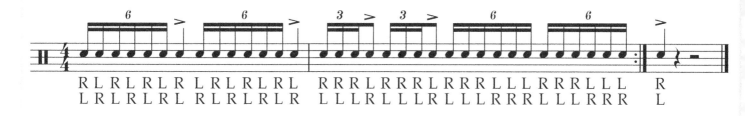

FRIDAY

Now let's review the Single Stroke Four and Triple Stroke Roll.

SATURDAY

Make sure to practice this exercise with your metronome!

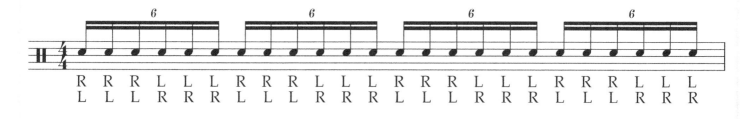

Be cautious with this sticking!

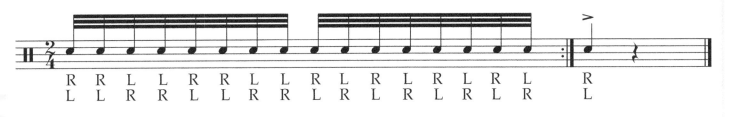

WEEK 47 SUMMARY EXERCISE

Watch your stickings with this exercise!

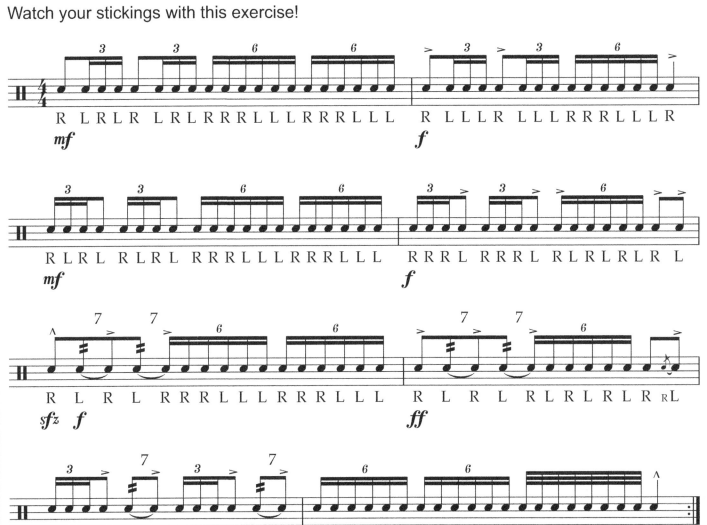

WEEK 48: MULTIPLE STROKE ROLL REVIEW

MONDAY

Make sure to practice moving to the edge of the drum and back.

TUESDAY

Count this syncopation on the "and" of beats 2 and 3.

WEDNESDAY

Today's exercise is a simple roll review. Work on your multiple-bounce sound!

THURSDAY

Here are some offbeat rolls.

FRIDAY

Make sure to count to the "and" of beat 3.

SATURDAY

Here's another exercise in shading toward the edge of the drum.

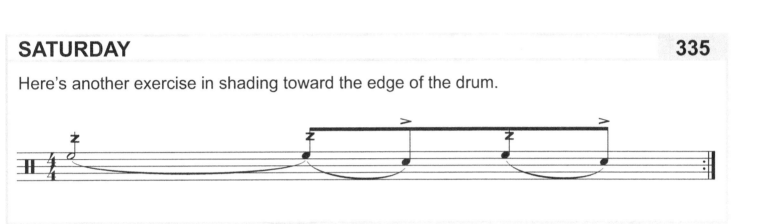

SUNDAY

Here's syncopation on the "and" of beat 1.

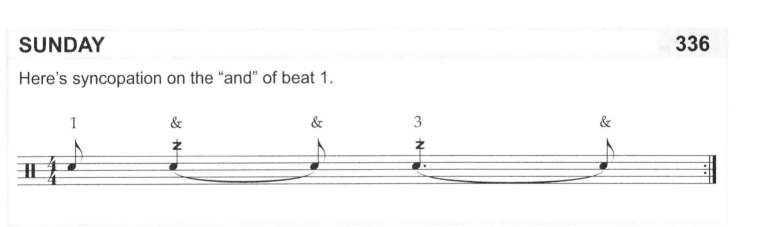

WEEK 48 SUMMARY EXERCISE

Make sure to play all the dynamics, shading, and an even-handed roll throughout this exercise.

WEEK 49: DOUBLE STROKE ROLL REVIEW

MONDAY

This exercise is a mix of the Five Stroke and Seven Stroke Roll.

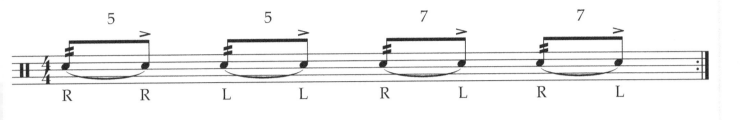

TUESDAY

Today, we combine the Seven Stroke and Nine Stroke Roll.

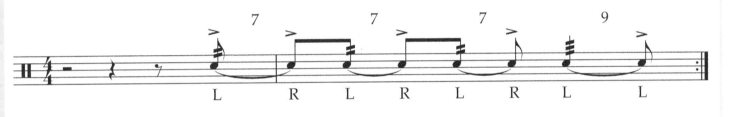

WEDNESDAY

Here, we mix of the Nine Stroke and Thirteen Stroke Roll.

THURSDAY

This exercise is a mix of the Nine Stroke Roll, Thirteen Stroke Roll, Five Stroke Roll, and Seven Stroke Roll.

FRIDAY

This exercise combines the Thirteen Stroke Roll, Nine Stroke Roll, and Six Stroke Roll.

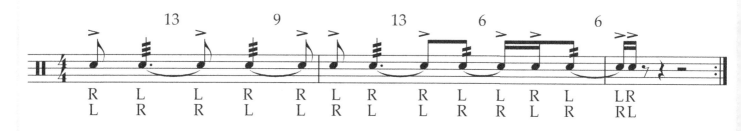

SATURDAY

Here, we have a mix of the Ten Stroke and Eleven Stroke Roll.

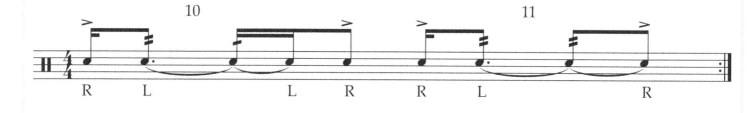

Our final exercise of the week is a mix of the Seventeen Stroke, Fifteen Stroke, Nine Stroke, and Thirteen Stroke Roll.

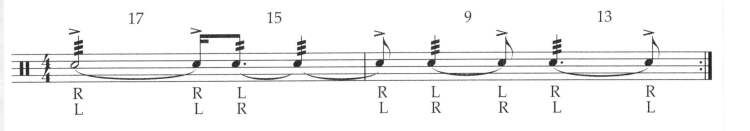

WEEK 49 SUMMARY EXERCISE

Make sure to count this summary exercise and play evenly with both hands.

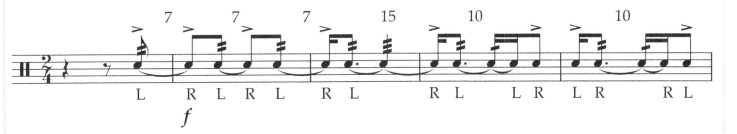

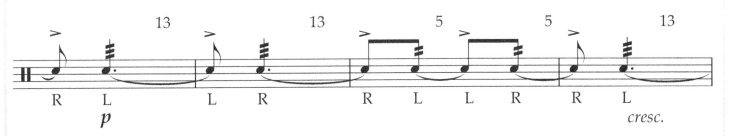

WEEK 50: FLAM RUDIMENT REVIEW

MONDAY

Today, we're going to review the Flam, Flam Paradiddle, Flamacue, and Flam Accent.

TUESDAY

Here's a review of the Flam Tap and the Pataflafla.

WEDNESDAY

This exercise is a review of the Flam Accent and the Flam Drag.

THURSDAY

Now let's review the Single Flammed Mill and the Flam Tap.

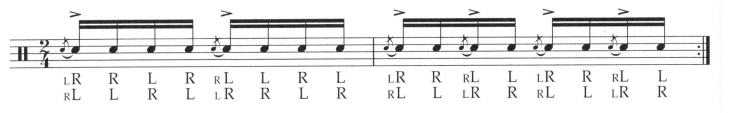

FRIDAY

Here's a review of the Swiss Army Triplet and the Inverted Flam Tap.

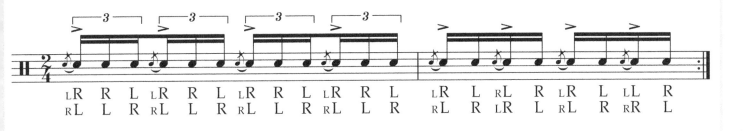

SATURDAY

Today, we're going to review the Inverted Flam Tap and the Flam Paradiddle-Diddle.

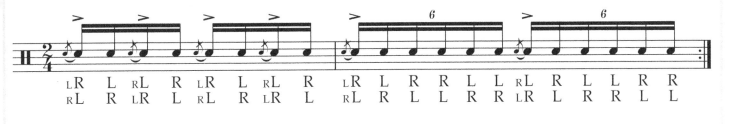

SUNDAY

This exercise is a review of the Swiss Army Triplet and the Flam Paradiddle-Diddle.

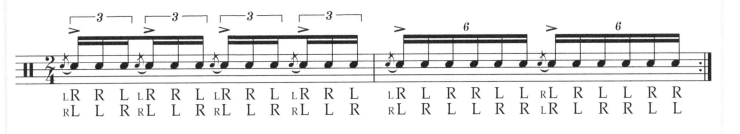

WEEK 50 SUMMARY EXERCISE

Make sure to play clean flams. Practice with a metronome and don't rush!

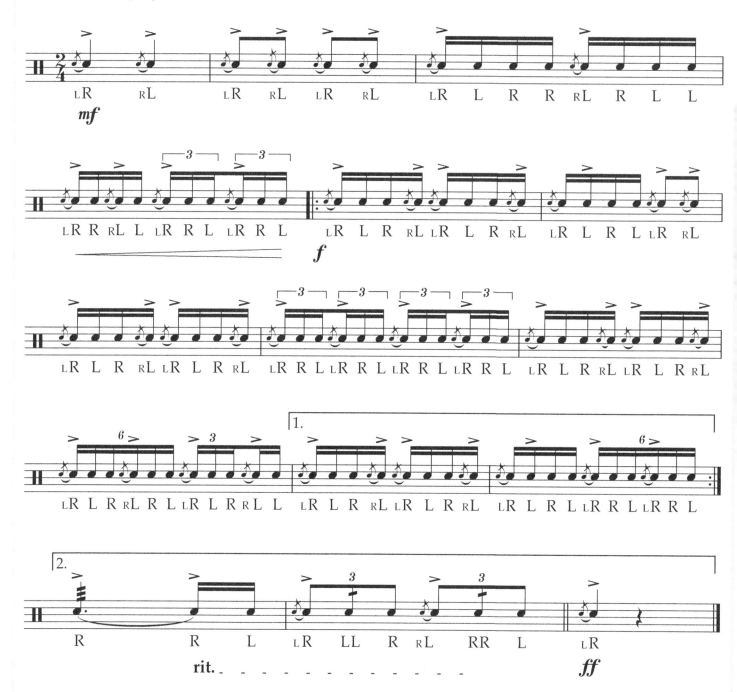

WEEK 51: DRAG RUDIMENT REVIEW

MONDAY

We'll start this week with a review of the Single Ratamacue and The Lesson 25.

TUESDAY

Here's a review of the Double Ratamacue and the Drag.

WEDNESDAY

Now let's review the Single Ratamacue and Triple Ratamacue.

THURSDAY

Today, we'll be reviewing Drag Paradiddle #1 and the Single Ratamacue.

FRIDAY

Here's a review exercise for the Single Drag and Single Ratamacue.

SATURDAY

This review exercise features the Singe Dragadiddle and Drag Paradiddle #2.

SUNDAY

We wrap up this week's exercises with a review of Drag Paradiddle #2 and the Syncopated Single Drag Tap.

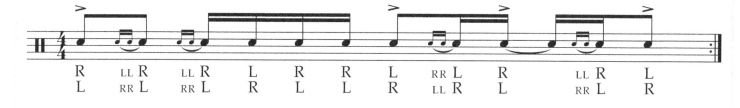

WEEK 51 SUMMARY EXERCISE

All right, we're ready for this summary exercise! Play all the figures cleanly.

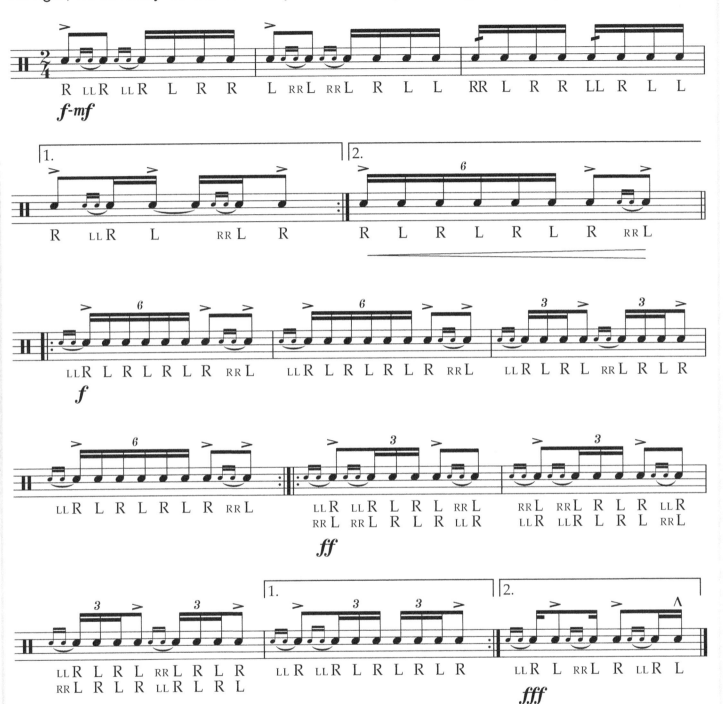

WEEK 52: MIXED TIME SIGNATURES REVIEW

MONDAY
358

Here, we have time signature changes that move between a quarter-note and an eighth-note pulse. Make sure to use a metronome to help with counting! In fact, write in the counting if you need to. This mixed-meter exercise combines 2/4 with 6/8 time signatures. Keep an even eighth-note pulse throughout.

TUESDAY
359

This mixed-meter example combines a measure of 5/4 and a measure of 7/8.

WEDNESDAY
360

Today's mixed-meter exercise combines a measure of 6/8 and a measure of 7/8.

THURSDAY
361

This mixed-meter example features two measures of 3/4 and one measure of 9/8.

FRIDAY

This mixed-meter exercise combines one measure of 12/8 and two measure of 2/4.

SATURDAY

Today's mixed-meter example links two measures of 3/8 with one measure of 5/4.

SUNDAY

Let's wrap up this week's exercises by combining some rudiments that move from 5/8 meter to 2/4 meter.

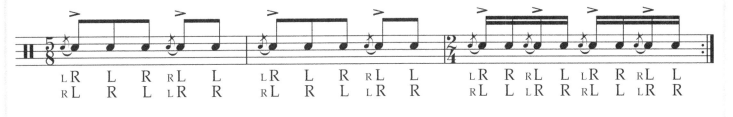

WEEK 52 SUMMARY EXERCISE

Here's a mixed-meter review exercise. Make sure to turn on the metronome and count! If you get stuck on the 5/8 section, review the exercise from Day 364, particularly the groups of 5.

DAY 365: MOVEMENT I

Today, you can dig into a snare drum solo! It may take you quite a bit longer than one day to master this solo but think of it as a reward for finishing the content of this book! Remember to count and to use dynamics and accents to perform musically. Have fun!

Performance Tip: If you have access to a concert drum and a parade drum, you can move to the parade drum for Movement II.

Andante

LR R L LR R L LR R L LR LLR R RL L   LR LLR L R R RL RRL R L L

1.

LR LLRLRL RRL RRLRLR L L R R L L

2.

LR LLRLRL RRL RRLRLR

fff

rit. _ _ _ _ _ _ _

ABOUT THE AUTHOR

Ben Hans is a percussionist, author, clinician, and music instructor based in Nashville, Tennessee. As an educator, Ben has taught private music lessons to students of all ages and skill levels for over three decades, including two decades as a collegiate music instructor.

Ben, who cut his teeth performing under the tutelage of jazz guitarist Jack Grassel and the late swing clarinetist Chuck Hedges, actively performs live in multiple music genres as a freelance artist. In addition to leading his own jazz trio, Ben has shared the stage with a diverse list of artists, including Kip Winger (acoustic); Eric Martin's BIG Acoustic; Trixter Acoustic (with Steve Brown and PJ Farley); Anthony Corder, the voice of Tora Tora; Ted Poley, the voice of Danger Danger; Tony Harnell, the voice of TNT; Danny Vaughn, the voice of Tyketto; Todd Kerns; Fiona Flanagan; Walter Egan; rock guitarists Reb Beach, John Roth, Donnie Wayne Smith, and Jorge Salán; Paul Taylor; Nashville singer-songwriters Doug Allen and Beth Sass; jazz pianist Barry Harris; jazz saxophonists Eric Morones, Johnny Padilla, Berkeley Fudge, and Jesse Lee Montijo; jazz guitarists Scott DuBois, Steve Peplin, Kirk Tatnall, Jeff Schroedl, Neil Davis, Michael Arnold, Michael Standal, and Pete Billman; jazz vocalist Jeannine Rivers; Swing Nouveau Big Band; blues artists Altered Five Blues Band, Jonny T-Bird and the MPs, and Tallan Noble Latz; percussionists John S. Pratt, Dominick Cuccia, Mitch Markovich, Jim Sewrey, Rick Embach, and Jeff Salisbury; as well as many more artists from many genres.

Ben is also a freelance author, editor, proofreader, and session performer, with published works that include *Workin' Drums: 50 Solos for Drumset*, *40 Intermediate Snare Drum Solos*, *Rudimental Drum Solos for the Marching Snare Drummer*, *Modern School for Mallet-Keyboard Instruments*, the *Hal Leonard School for Snare Drum*, *First 50 Solos You Should Play on the Snare Drum*, and *How to Play Drums in 14 Days*. Additionally, Ben transcribed the music for Ray Luzier's *Double Bass Drum Techniques* and was a writer, editor, musical director, and performer on the DVD *John S. Pratt: Traditional Rudimental Drumming*.

Ben is a Yamaha Performing Artist who also currently endorses Aquarian Drumheads, Vic Firth Drumsticks, Mike Balter Mallets, Impression Cymbals, and Tycoon Percussion. Ben is a member of ASCAP and John S. Pratt's International Association of Traditional Drummers. Have a question about this book, want an online lesson, or come to see a live show? For more information, visit his website: *benhans.com*.

Made in the USA
Monee, IL
22 November 2024

70929855R00092